In memory
of
Terry Twohig. RIP.

58 40

Journey

Journey
Spiritual Insights

by
Chiara Lubich

New City Press, New York

Published in the United States by New City Press
the Publishing House of the Focolare
206 Skillman Avenue, Brooklyn, NY 11211 ©1984 by New City
Press, New York
Translated from the original Italian edition
La vita, un viaggio ©1984 Citta' Nuova Editrice, Rome, Italy
by Hugh J. Moran and William D. Hartnett

Cover design by Tommaso Gianotta
Library of Congress Catalog Number: 84-61268
ISBN 0-911782-51-6
Printed in the United States of America

Nihil Obstat: Michael J. Curran, S.T.L., Delegated Censor
Imprimatur: Francis J. Mugavero, D.D., Bishop of Brooklyn
Brooklyn, N.Y., October 10, 1984

CONTENTS

Some Focolare Terms

The following brief definitions may prove helpful to those readers who are not familiar with the Focolare.

Focolare: An Italian word meaning "hearth," "family fireside." It was the name given to the initial group by others who felt the "warmth" of their love. Focolare refers to the Focolare Movement as a whole, also known as the Work of Mary.

Focolare household: A small community of either men or women, who have vows of poverty, chastity, and obedience, whose first aim is to achieve among themselves the unity Jesus prayed for, through the practice of mutual love. There are also married members, who live with their families.

focolarina: A member of a women's focolare household. Plural: *focolarine.*

focolarino: A member of a men's focolare household. Plural: *focolarini* (also used to indicate *focolarine* and *focolarini* collectively).

volunteer: The volunteers—short for "Volunteers for God"—are members of the Focolare who are particularly committed to bringing the Gospel spirit to bear on the relationships and structures of society at large.

gen: Gen is short for "New Generation"; and the Gen Movement is the new generation of the Focolare. A gen is an individual member of the Gen Movement. The gens are young people committed to living the Gospel message of love and unity, and to sharing it with other youth.

Mariapolis: Literally, City of Mary. This is the name given to the large annual gathering of members and friends of the Focolare. Permanent Mariapolises are small towns where young people, families, priests, and religious from different countries live and work together. Mariapolis Centers are meeting centers for members and friends of the Focolare.

Centro Uno: The Focolare secretariat for ecumenical activities, located in Rome.

Ideal: The word Ideal is used in the Focolare, primarily to mean God, chosen as the one aim in life. Secondly, it also stands for the Focolare spirituality and the way it is lived in daily life.

INTRODUCTION

As Pope Paul VI pointed out in 1974, people today are more willing to listen to experience than to statements of theory. This is especially true of the younger generation. They've seen so many shattered myths, that they instinctively reject any talk about theories, and look for something genuine and practical. Paul VI's words encourage Christians to renew their efforts at presenting a genuine "incarnation" of the Gospel. Despite the increasing signs of decadence around us, the new springtime in the Church, already forseen by Pius XII in 1958, is more visible than ever.

Sanctity seems to have become relevant to more categories of people, now that Vatican II has reasserted that it is the vocation of all Christians. Although they're not making lots of headlines, we are hearing more and more about people trying to live heroic Christian lives. We find them among politicians, simple working people, family members, students, people with health problems, and the list goes on. They're youths and married folks, mothers and fathers, well-educated and simple people — lay people who have clearly understood the role of the People of God, and are trying to carry out that role as best they can.

As a result, an ever larger number of Christians are focusing their attention on the movements that the Holy Spirit has raised up in abundance to answer the needs of his Church. The Focolare is among these and is now present all over the world. It began during World War II, as a result of Chiara Lubich's powerful rediscovery that God is love. She was at once followed by a sizeable group of youths, and then by many other people from different backgrounds and walks of life.

The Focolare works for unity—the fullest expression of Christian love—to fulfill the prayer of Jesus, "That all may be one" (Jn. 17:21). One of its characteristic features is the deep communion among its members, based on the sharing of their spiritual experiences. This is an essential feature of their type of spirituality, which is "collective" by its very nature. The Focolare members speak of spiritual life as a journey towards God *together*.

This book reflects their effort to journey forward together. It incorporates the spiritual thoughts that the author shared (about once every two weeks, from September 1981 to February 1984) with people of the Focolare, during conference calls linking forty locations around the world—from Brazil to Australia, to the United States, to Kenya, to Chile, to Japan, as well as various places in Europe.

These spiritual thoughts, which were followed by "family news" during the phone calls, merit being offered to others beyond those for whom they were originally intended. They are truly profound, and effectively insist upon fundamental points of Christian life.

One of the recurring refrains in these writings is the *Word of Life*, a common and well-rooted practice in the Focolare. Living according to the Word of Life is a bond of unity among the Focolare members, and a guiding light for the evangelization of their daily lives. The practice of the Word of Life, which is also spreading among Christians at large, provides a practical way to understand and live the message of Jesus.

Another underlying theme in these writings is the urgency of getting to the "precious pearl" of the Gospel—mutual love—so as to merit the name of Christian: "I give you a new commandment, that you love one another as I have loved you. By this will all know that you are my disciples, that you love one another" (Jn. 13:34-35). And yet another theme is the indispensable love for the cross, which is the common denominator of every authentic spirituality in the Church. And with this, the new insight of the Focolare: its particular love for Jesus Forsaken.

The general background against which these "thoughts" with their various themes develop is a pilgrimage, *the Holy Journey* of life. This is the living out of the Christian vocation "to be perfect as the Father" (cf. Mt. 5:48)—the continuous striving toward God as members of the Church. The numerous references to this divine adventure are vividly described, the images used often reflecting the input of the younger members of the Focolare.

The author's style is straight and to the point. Speaking to persons of various cultures and educational levels, including people in the mocambos (shanty towns) of Recife and the barrios (slums) of Manila, she is always coming up with new ideas to stimulate her listeners to go deeper into the spiritual life. She frequently sums up her message in a catchy motto. Her language is warm, familiar, conversational, rich in metaphor, and reminiscent of many of the great spiritual writers down through the centuries. Her writing has been compared at times to the writings of St. Teresa of Avila. But, above all, what she says has a lot in common with the Gospels' themselves, where the lessons are drawn from the events of everyday life.

What we have here could be likened to a modern version of the collected letters of some of the great spiritual writers of earlier times—filled with spiritual advice which is the fruit of experience. Also noteworthy are the references Lubich makes to certain passages of St. John of the Cross, evidence of how her own Christian experience has led her to appreciate the value of other manifestations of the Spirit in the Church and to treasure them as her own.

In light of what has been said, we are certain that this little volume has much to offer to a great number of people.

"Blessed are those whose strength is in you,
who have set their hearts on pilgrimage."

(Ps: 84:5 NIV)

1981

Uppermost in my mind today is a desire for us *focolarini* to take a closer look at how we are doing in terms of our commitment to reach sanctity. A few days ago a *focolarina* brought to my attention a beautiful sentence from the Psalms, that proclaims a beatitude I'd never heard of: "Blessed are those whose strength is in you, who have set their hearts on pilgrimage" (Ps. 84:5 NIV).

"Pilgrimage?" What pilgrimage is Scripture speaking about? Our journey toward Heaven and God, of course; and thus, our journey toward sanctity, which will lead us to Heaven. All of us *focolarini* made a decision to undertake this Holy Journey when we said "yes" to our vocation. In fact, since our lives are consecrated to God, we have an even greater obligation to strive for spiritual perfection than other people do. So then, have we really set out on this Holy Journey? In this present moment, are we moving onward?

Today is the 246th day of 1981, the 246th day since we made a more conscious decision to strive for sanctity, motivated by the example of Sister Maria Gabriella, the Trappistine nun.[1] Two hundred and forty-six days! Let's each pause a moment and put ourselves before God; and for his glory alone, let's take stock of the situation.

Have there been any results? Have we improved, for instance, in doing God's will? Are we any better at loving? What about our mutual love? Are we better at denying ourselves and at practicing mortification? In other words, have we improved at loving Jesus Forsaken? If the answer is yes, then let's give thanks to God and get on with it. If the answer is no, let's thank God that we still have time to start afresh. Then, onward! We really want to experience the happiness of those who set their hearts on the Holy Journey!

Rocca di Papa, September 3, 1981

DECLARE WAR ON OUR WILL

So we have set out on our Holy Journey! The recurring theme among us here these last few days has been: *Declare war on our will*, since to go forward in this Holy Journey we must do God's will. So let's all live each succeeding present moment, trying to do away with our will so as to root ourselves firmly in God's will.

Now only one hundred and five days remain in this year characterized by our common thrust toward sanctity. May all these days — or as many as God gives us — be completely his! This is my wish: that we may actually succeed in becoming saints, and that we may each be able to present our sanctity to our Blessed Mother through the hands of our guardian angel. With this bright prospect before us, let's keep these resolutions we have made!

Rocca di Papa, September 17, 1981

THE WATCHWORD: CUT

Now we are all racing forward! We have only three months left before the end of this year in which we have all committed ourselves to go toward sanctity together. The Blessed Mother, who seems to want to satisfy our desire to reach sanctity, has been leading us along the way of Christian asceticism. We know what *our* asceticism is: to love our neighbor perfectly; because in making ourselves one with others we die to ourselves. But Jesus knew that we would not always have neighbors around to love. That is why he speaks about denying ourselves, sometimes using very strong language. Recently, I was very struck by his words, "If your hand or foot is your undoing, cut it off and throw it from you! Better to enter life maimed or crippled than be thrown with two hands or two feet into endless fire" (Mt. 18:8).

What could he mean? He wants to show us how strongly he feels that we must get rid of everything that interferes with our relationship with him. He is challenging us not only to avoid serious evil, but to wipe out every attachment to anything but him.

And so we return to the idea of "cutting," "bombarding," giving up, doing away with, "declaring war" on everything that is not he, that is not his will in the present moment. This is what we have to do! Let's love Jesus Forsaken in this cutting and losing, so that he can be our only love.
The watchword for the next two weeks is obvious: *cut*. If anything interferes with our loving God or doing his will, let's get rid of it!

Rocca di Papa, October 1, 1981

ENKINDLE FIRES OF LOVE EVERYWHERE

What I want to focus on today is unity. Unity must triumph—unity with God, unity among all people. The way to achieve this is to love everyone with that merciful love which characterized the Focolare at its beginnings, when we decided that each morning and all through the day we would look upon every person we met—at home, at school, at work, everywhere—as a new person, brand new, deliberately not remembering any of his or her short-comings or defects, but covering everything over with love. That is precisely how this month's Word of Life[2] invites us to love: to forgive seventy times seven times; to reach out to everyone we meet with complete "amnesty," universal pardon, in our hearts; and then to "make ourselves one" with them in everything except sin and evil.

Why should we do this? To obtain the same wonderful results the Apostle Paul was seeking when he said: "Al-though I am not bound to anyone, I made myself the slave of all so as to win over as many as possible.... I have made myself all things to all men" (1 Cor. 9:19,22). If we "make ourselves one" with our neighbor, as Paul recommends, which will be easier when we have this forgiving attitude, we will be able to pass our "Ideal" on to others.[3] And once this has been accomplished we can have Jesus present among us,[4] the risen Jesus who promised to remain with us forever in his Church, and who allows us to almost see and hear him when he is in our midst.

This must be our principle work: to live in such a way that Jesus may live among us—Jesus, who is victorious over the world. For if we are one, as time goes on many will be one, and the world will someday be able to witness unity.

So let's create cells of unity everywhere, each a *"focolare,"* burning with love: in our family, on our block, with our playmates, with the people at work or at school—with everyone we can. Let's enkindle fires of love everywhere!

This is where we must concentrate our greatest efforts. Loving like this, to the point of having Jesus in our midst, demands sacrifice, mortification, detachment, giving things up, and "dropping bombs" on our own will so we can do our neighbor's will. We want to give the Focolare around the world a new look: We want to see fires of love enkindled everywhere, so that everywhere Jesus may be in our midst. If, with his grace, we do our part to have him living among us, he will make the most beautiful virtues blossom in our hearts.

During the next two weeks, then, let's concentrate on this: *to enkindle fires of love everywhere* by "making ourselves one."

Rocca di Papa, October 15, 1981

PREPARE TO LOVE BY EMBRACING
PERSONAL SUFFERING

We have only fifty-six days left in this wonderful year during which many, many of us have set out on the Holy Journey, confidently casting aside any doubts and second thoughts. At the year's end we will balance the accounts and see what progress we have made with the help of God's grace and for his glory. In the meantime, the remaining days that God gives to us should be considered precious, because they are an opportunity for us to regain any lost ground.

We want to become saints—but all together. So let's see what we should work toward between now and the next conference call.[5] The particular aspect of God's will for us that we are stressing during this year is unity, our specific goal. Each month we also have a Word of Life, taken from the liturgical readings, which we try to make an integral part of our lives. November's Word of Life is: "Happy those who mourn: they shall be comforted" (Mt. 5:4 JB).

How can we focus our lives on unity and, at the same time, on the Word of Life? By using our daily efforts to live the Word of Life as a means to bring about unity. In other words, living the Word of Life in function of unity. Let me explain. The Word of Life says: "Happy those who mourn: they shall be comforted." We should experience the happiness and consolation these words promise. Suffering *is* worthwhile! We must always, immediately, and joyfully embrace the daily sufferings that come our way, as well as the suffering that results when we stifle our own stubborn ego. If we do this, the suffering will be transformed into joy, peace, consolation. And if we are at peace, we will be able to love everyone we meet. We will feel free, and be able to "make ourselves one" with them, thus living for unity.

In short, let's willingly *embrace our personal sufferings so we will be ready to love our neighbor*. Let this be our common goal for the next two weeks. Now let's get to work!

Rome, November 5, 1981

MAKE REPARATION SO WE CAN LOVE BETTER

We have eleven days left till the end of November, in which we should be living according to the Word of Life "Happy those who mourn: for they shall be comforted" (Mt. 5:4 JB), and sharing our experiences of doing it. So during these days let's do this the best we can, taking full advantage of the rich, divine meaning of these words. We know that God's words are not like human words. He himself is present in them, as the Word "uttered" by the Father from all eternity. Thus by nourishing ourselves on God's word, we nourish ourselves on God. We receive light, with which we can also enlighten others; and love, which besides warming our hearts, can also inflame the hearts of others.

How are we to live according to this Word of Life? I think that if Jesus calls "happy" or "blest" those who are afflicted with suffering they have not sought but are simply faced with, then those who seek suffering for love of God, to follow Jesus and to progress more quickly on the Holy Journey, are certainly also blest—perhaps even more blest. There are many things that being a disciple of Jesus demands of us, that are painful, that are "afflictions" for our ego: self-denial, for example; giving up whatever is not God's will; "cuts"; detachment; and so on. I would like to suggest one for these next eleven days of our Holy Journey.

Someone told me once that no one ever became a saint without having practiced some form of penance. So my suggestion for living according to the Word of Life is this: every time we notice that we have done something wrong, let's do some act of penance to make reparation for the good that we failed to do. Here are some examples: If we have been irritable with our neighbor, if we have offended him or judged him harshly, let's try to make up for it by being twice as nice, by pointing out his good points to others, by sticking up for him if necessary, unmindful of whatever wrong he might have done, as if nothing at all had ever happened. Or if we have eaten more than we needed, let's make up for it by cutting down at our next meal, offering this to Jesus. If we find we have been inattentive while praying, as if we were not really speaking to anyone, let's recollect ourselves for a moment of really intense prayer; and so on. There are thousands and thousands of ways to make reparation.

I have been trying to do this myself, and I assure you that it brings joy and peace to your heart. You have the impression that, for that moment at least, you are in union with God. And with this peace in your heart, it is easier to live in unity. Love of neighbor becomes easier, as does "living the other person," as we say, and "making ourselves one" with our neighbor, whom we must serve; like Jesus, who even though he was Lord and Master, washed his disciples' feet.

To sum up: *let's make reparation so we can love better.*

Rocca di Papa, November 19, 1981

It's the last month of the year. From your letters, telegrams, and messages, I have seen that some of you, who had not yet come to a decision about the Holy Journey, have climbed on board "the train," as our gens say, ready to continue the journey with everyone else who receives this conference call.

What can I tell you today? Just a few days ago I saw some very young athletes, most of them from Eastern Europe, who were performing wonderful gymnastic feats. The way they did those somersaults, spins, and other moves, was just magnificent! What perfection! What harmony and grace! They were in perfect command of their bodies, so much so that the most difficult exercises seemed to come naturally. They are the world champions.

Several times while I was watching them, I felt I was being given a challenge, perhaps by the Holy Spirit. It was as if someone were telling me: *"You too, all of you, must become world champions. Champions at what? Champions at loving God. Do you know how much these gymnasts have had to practice? Do you know that day after day, for hours and hours at a time, they repeat the same movements over and over again, without ever giving up? You too, all of you, will have to do the same. When? In each and every present moment, without ever giving up."* And I began to have an overwhelming desire to become perfect at loving God in each present moment.

St. Francis de Sales says that no one has such natural goodness that he or she cannot be corrupted by repeated acts of vice. Conversely, we might say that no one is so corrupt that he or she cannot become virtuous by repeated acts of virtue. So don't be afraid! If we practice, we will become world champions at loving God.

This month's Word of Life says: "I am the handmaid of the Lord. Let it be done to me according to your word" (Lk. 1:38 RSV). We too, like Mary, must say: "Let it be done to me according to your word." The word that God has said to the Focolare is *unity*. Therefore, we must become *champions at unity*: being one with God and with his will in each present moment, and being one with our neighbor, every neighbor we meet during the day.

Come on then! Let's start practicing, and not waste a single precious minute! What awaits us is not merely a gold medal, but Heaven itself. And because of the Communion of Saints, many others will benefit from our actions.

Rocca di Papa, December 3, 1981

ALLOW JESUS TO BE BORN IN OUR MIDST

In a few days, it will be Christmas. And before I speak with you again, the first year of our determined effort to reach sanctity together will have come to a close. As you know, Christmas reminds us of an essential point of our spirituality, which is also a basic norm that characterizes our Focolare way of life. Actually, more than a point or a norm, it is a reality, a great reality that we are called to offer the world: Jesus in our midst. Jesus is born among us if we love one another with a love that is ever new. In fact, to *allow Jesus to be born in our midst* is our first obligation, the basic reason for the Focolare's existence.

Perhaps that is why the following thought has been running through my mind lately. It is a kind of admonition: "You cannot allow yourself the luxury of becoming a saint unless *the* Saint is in your midst. Don't fool yourself into thinking that you can reach Christian perfection if the One who is perfect is not among you."

What are we to do then? I think we must try to have Jesus among us and try to keep him with us, by having a love for one another that is characterized by a spirit of service and of understanding, that wants to share the sufferings, burdens, cares, and joys of the other; a typically Christian love, that covers everything over, that always forgives. We should try to be sure that the Risen Lord, who promised to be with his Church until the end of time, is among us as a result of our mutual love. And then we should do God's will in each succeeding moment, as perfectly as we can, absolutely refusing to listen to our own will.

This is what we should do during these last two weeks of the year, in line with the Word of Life, which urges us to do God's will as Mary did. God's will for us is similar to God's will for her: it is first and foremost to give life to Jesus. In this way we will really become champions at unity with God and with our neighbor.

Have a blessed Christmas then; and remember that Jesus can be present among us even if we are far from one another.

Tokyo, December 17, 1981

1982

LIGHTED CANDLES

1982 has begun! We have completed one year of our Holy Journey. Thanks be to God! I hope that as a result of our efforts to reach sanctity we were all able to offer a hymn of praise to God, because we had fewer sins and more numerous acts of love.

Now let's step on the gas! Here are two of the New Year's resolutions I and those here with me have made. The ideas for them came to us here in the Far East. First: We all want to become "locomotives." Many gens have drawn or constructed model trains to represent the Holy Journey. Frequently, my name gets put on the locomotive. Of course, God knows who is really moving the train. It is undoubtedly those who are doing the most loving. In any case, this image prompted us to formulate a resolution: this year, none of the forty-three thousand[6] of us who are on the Holy Journey can allow ourselves to be just ordinary cars in the train. We must all be locomotives! How can we do this? By drawing at least one other person along with us in this race toward God. This is our first resolution.

Now for the second. In our contacts with our Buddhist brothers and sisters, we learned that one of their symbols is the extinguished candle. It signifies complete mortification, total absence of desires. We really have to admire them for the way they put this into practice. We Christians, instead, have a lighted candle, because Jesus brought us grace and divine life. He enkindled a flame in our hearts, which enables us to carry out our duty to love God and our neighbor by doing God's will one-hundred percent in each present moment, and by making ourselves one with our neighbor. In this way, the worldliness within us dies; our desires and passions are silenced. And so we have our second resolution: To be *lighted candles*.

Hongkong, January 7, 1982

EVERYONE WITH A CLUSTER

In our last conference call we decided that for the new year we would not be simply cars in the train, but locomotives pulling others along. If we do this, we will find ourselves grouped in clusters,[7] as we have been stressing recently.

I was very pleased to see during this rapid visit to the Focolare communities in Asia, how they take things seriously, and immediately put them into practice. This was typified by a gen in Hongkong, who came up to one of us after a wonderful meeting and said: "I'd like you to meet my cluster." Thereupon, he introduced her to several other young people with whom he tries to live our Ideal by keeping in touch with them, and loving and serving them so they can become saints together. Then he added: "Now I'd like you to meet the person whose cluster I belong to." And he introduced him to her.

I wish that all of us could be like that gen, that we could introduce ourselves as part of a cluster — not only when we meet one another; but when we present ourselves before God, both now and at the end of our lives. I would also like all of us to imitate those wonderful volunteers from a nucleus in Manila, who welcomed me on my arrival here with a big poster. In this equatorial climate, not only do grapes come in bunches, but so do many other fruits, like coconuts, mangos, bananas, mangosteens, and so on. At the center of the volunteers' poster was a group picture of themselves, all of them with cheerful and confident faces. Around the photograph were their signatures, each with a different cluster represented by a different bunch of fruit.

That is how we should all be. That is what we must work on for the next two weeks. Let's not make God the Father have to ask: "And where are your brothers and sisters?"

Tagaytay, Philippines, January 21, 1982

KEEP GOING FORWARD

Our Holy Journey continues, and we cannot pause, much less start going backwards. Jesus said: "Whoever puts his hand to the plow but keeps looking back is unfit for the reign of God" (Lk. 9:62). Here in Australia, the coat of arms of this young country reminds us of this, because it depicts two animals, chosen precisely because they can't walk backwards: the kangaroo and the emu, an Australian bird.

We, too, must *keep going forward* courageously. And to guide us on our way we have the Word of Life, which is "A lamp to my feet ... a light to my path" (Ps. 119:105). This month's Word of Life is: "To the weak I became a weak person with a view to winning the weak. I have made myself all things to all men in order to save at least some of them" (1 Cor. 9:22). We should have a special love for this Word of Life because it reminds us of how we must act if we want to follow the way of unity and contribute to the fulfillment of Jesus' prayer, "That all may be one" (Jn. 17:21). We must "make ourselves one" with every neighbor. We know this is the way, because it is the way chosen by God himself to show us his love. He became a human being like ourselves and let himself be crucified and forsaken, to put himself at everyone's level. He really made himself weak with the weak! And thus he opened the way so that all may be one. He bent down to our level; but he did not break. Just like the bamboo, that is used for so many things in the Philippines, because it bends without breaking.

We are called to contribute to the fulfillment of Jesus' prayer for unity. So first of all, let's renew our faith that every human being is called to unity, since God loves everyone. And let's not try to find excuses, such as: "That person will never understand!" "That one's too young to understand"; "That's one of my relatives. I know him only too well! He's too attached to the things of this world"; "That person's superstitious and believes in spiritism"; "That one belongs to another religion"; "That one's too old to change." Enough of these judgements! God loves everyone, and is there waiting for them. The only thing we have to do is love each and every person, by serving them and by making ourselves completely one with them in everything but sin. Let Jesus worry about winning them over! And he will; if not now, in ten, or twenty, or thirty years. But he will! I know from experience.

In conclusion, for the next two weeks let's take a closer look at all our relationships, and work at making ourselves one with each person. In this way we will be ensuring that our efforts for unity will be effective.

Melbourne, February 2, 1982

ENLARGE THE CIRCLE

Today we have another idea that can encourage us on the Holy Journey we have undertaken together and which is leading us—with God's help and for his sole glory—toward our collective sanctification. To guide us on our Journey, we have the light of God's word. *God's word!* But do we realize what God's word is? I am always struck by the comparison Scripture makes between God's word and ourselves: "All flesh is grass and its beauty like the wild flower's. The grass withers, the flower fades, but the word of our God remains forever" (Is. 40: 6,8JB).

We ought to have a great respect for God's word. But looking at how we treat it, we see that we are frequently limited by our own narrow conception of it: we think we already know it; or we think it doesn't apply to our case, and so we dismiss it; or we live according to it for a while, and then think we have used it up. In any case, we certainly never appreciate it for what it's worth. But the fact is that we will pass away, and it will remain. Jesus' words will never pass away.

What we should do, then, is try to have the right idea about God's word. We should regard it as a presence of Christ, which it is; and we should feel honored to be able to live according to it, to "clothe ourselves" with it in each present moment. This month's Word of Life continues to repeat to us: "To the weak I became a weak person with a view to winning the weak. I have made myself all things to all men in order to save at least some of them" (1 Cor. 9:22).

Someone asked me: "How far should I go in "making myself one," in loving and serving each neighbor with the hope of reaching unity sooner or later?" Jesus himself gives us the answer. He "made himself one" with us by becoming a human being. Then he experienced the same weariness and suffering that we experience. He even went so far as to die. He experienced everything that is a part of our human condition, except sin.

Only if we "make ourselves one" as he did, will our Christian love be blest and fruitful. Many will then respond to our love, and the circle of those around us who want to have God as their Ideal will get larger and larger; like the ripples around a stone thrown into the water. This was also Paul's idea in "making himself one": "I have made myself the slave of all so as to win over as many as possible" (1 Cor. 9:19).

Let's get going then! Let's *enlarge the circle* of God's kingdom!

Rocca di Papa, February 18, 1982

Here we are—now and for the rest of our lives, we hope—on the Holy Journey which we have all set out on together. And certainly we are not doing this because we have a mania to be perfect, or to nourish our spiritual pride. Neither are we doing it to be better than others; but we are doing it to be holy for the glory of God, because God wants it. In fact, St. Paul says, "It is God's will that you grow in holiness" (1 Thess 4:3). So then, during these next two weeks: *Forward! Forward, without stopping!* And if in the past we have stopped, as can happen and does happen, then we have one more reason for setting out anew with added vigor on the Holy Journey.

"Be holy," Mother Teresa one day wrote to me, "because Jesus is holy." And that's the way it is: we must become holy, which means become saints, because Jesus is holy. And we become saints by living God's word. We know that whoever is living according to his word, is already holy, at least in that moment. Jesus said, "Those who listen to my word" (that is, those who receive his word in their heart and put it into practice) "are already made clean" (cf. Jn. 15:3). If this is true, then it is clear that we will become saints by trying our best to be God's word, God's living word in every moment—including right now.

Today we want to understand better how to live according to God's word. We should regard living according to his word as the most important thing we have to do in our lives. How many times our heart is drawn, instead, toward the many things there are in the world around us, or to-

ward those things which are within us. And how often, for
example, we give first place to our job, to our apostolic
work, to our studies, or perhaps even to a hobby or to
amusements. Oftentimes we are dominated by vanity or
chained by affections, and sometimes we are even slaves of
things which are not at all pleasing to God. So, practically
speaking, most of the time we direct our mind's attention,
our heart's affection, and the thrust of our will towards the
things of this earth.

What place does God's word occupy in our lives? Well,
we remember it every so often, and that's it. But this is not
the kind of life that Jesus expects of us. God's word must
be our first love, before everything else. It must be the
pillar which supports our entire life, the root from which
the rest of our life blossoms. It is his word which must
enlighten our every activity, moment by moment. It must
straighten out and correct every aspect of our life.

Look at Mary: her life was all in conformity with the
words of God, which she kept in her heart and meditated
on, so as to translate them into life. We might say that
Mary is totally *Word of God*, and since she lived holiness
perfectly, her life was really a Holy Journey.

But let us look above all at Jesus. He lived just as we do.
He was a carpenter, he worked hard, he was active in doing
apostolic work. He rested, he ate, he loved Mary and Jo-
seph. He instructed his disciples, he worked miracles, he
fed the masses. But who was Jesus? Wasn't he the Word,
the Word of God made flesh?

Since Jesus, the Word of God, took upon Himself our
human nature, we will be true Christians and become
saints if we allow the whole of our lives to be permeated
with God's word.

The Word of Life that we are considering this month is:
"If anyone wants to serve me, let him follow me, and where

I am, there will my servant be. If anyone serves me, my Father will honor him" (Jn. 12:26). And we know that following Jesus means to deny ourselves and to embrace the cross. Every goal we want to reach takes discipline, sacrifice, sweat, practice; and it is the same with Christian perfection. Self-denial and the cross are hard words, but we know that the Holy Journey is demanding. And besides, that's what Christianity is: to live the death of Jesus so that he can rise in us moment by moment. Therefore, let's prune away our old self, so that the tree of our life will not remain a useless little shrub, but instead will give tasty fruit. We don't want to wait until the last moment of our lives, when our death has already become inevitable, to offer it to God. No, love for him tells us to die day by day, with his help, so as to rise again day by day, moment by moment.

Sierre, March 15, 1982

IS EVERYTHING TAKEN CARE OF?

The Word of Life for April says to us, "If I have washed your feet—I who am Teacher and Lord—then you must wash each other's feet" (Jn. 13:14).The radicalness of these words reminded me of an episode that happened several years ago, which impressed me deeply. A young mother of ten children, struck by cancer, had entrusted her children one by one to various families. When she felt that death was approaching, she set out to visit all of her children for the last time. The journey was long and very tiring. When she had completed this last obligation, as she returned to her sickbed, she said: *"Everything is taken care of."*

This mother teaches us what love truly is. God has also entrusted us with persons to be loved, taken care of, and helped; so that we might travel together on this Holy Journey of life the best way possible, and pay our debt of love.

The last time we spoke together, we understood that we had to be God's living word. What can we do now, to incarnate as perfectly as possible this month's splendid Word of Life, in which Jesus gives us an unparalleled example of the way Christians ought to love?

I think that a good system would be to examine ourselves every evening, to see if we too, like that mother, can say with reference to those who have been entrusted to us: *"Everything is taken care of."* This might mean we have given them some help, some advice, a gift, or a simple smile; that we have shared their burden, misfortune, or joy; that we have shared our food, or clothing, or money; that we have shared a beautiful and useful idea to help us get ahead in the Holy Journey.

Christianity is love. God demands this loving service of us. But he does not demand it of us only as individuals. This month's Word of Life tells us clearly that this way of loving must be reciprocal. In fact, Jesus says, "...you must also wash one another's feet."

On my recent trip to Holland, I was struck, among other things, by the motto of this nation, which says: "In concord small things become great." This is so true, and Holland, in its constant struggle to wrest land from the sea, must have experienced this truth many times. Jesus wants his followers to be of one heart, too. In fact, he demands even more: mutual love, which should be the basis of their whole life. It is that love which makes everything else we do worthwhile, which causes his presence to blossom in our midst. He knows how to use even our own small lives to work miracles of love. And he will make us experience that blessing he proclaimed after washing the apostles' feet, when he said: "What I just did was to give you an example: as I have done, so you must do.... Once you know all these things, blest will you be if you put them into practice" (Jn. 13:15,17).

Rome, April 1, 1982

We have just lived the important days of Holy Week, and my heart is still filled with the great themes which Holy Week has reminded us of: the New Commandment, with the washing of the feet; the institution of the priesthood on Holy Thursday, the day Pope Paul VI chose to celebrate the ministerial priesthood and the royal priesthood of all the faithful; the institution of the Eucharist; the Testament of Jesus; Jesus' passion and abandonment on Good Friday; and his resurrection on Easter, which this year as never before we felt was our special feast.

These are all such extraordinary, supernatural things, that it is very difficult to leave them behind now. It is almost as if we wished that our whole life could be one long Holy Week. These are all events which Christians are called to live out every day of their lives; and not only every day, but every moment. In fact, if we want our lives to be a Holy Journey, we must die to ourselves every day, in every moment, so as to rise in him.

So how can we live in such a way that these realities may always be present in our lives, so that these immense gifts can bear as much fruit as possible?

I intend to suggest three ways, which can be summed up in one. First of all, during these next two weeks, let's set our hearts on our one great love: Jesus crucified and forsaken. Let's love him first of all, in sufferings, embracing them always, immediately, and joyfully, repeating in the face of suffering the words that Danilo, our volunteer from Stockholm, repeated with such conviction just a short time before he left for the Heavenly Mariapolis[8]: "Everything is love — everything!"

Let's also love him by immersing ourselves in God's will in each present moment, forgetting our own will, which we don't want to take into consideration. Finally, let us love him by making ourselves one with every neighbor we meet—perfectly one in everything except sin. This demands dying to ourselves.

I assure you that if we live like this, we will lose nothing of what Holy Week has given us and reminded us of. "Washing one another's feet" will become our way of life. And consequently, so will the New Commandment. The Testament of Jesus will come true. We will live out our royal priesthood in all its fullness, which will be a wonderful and fruitful support for those who have the ministerial priesthood.

The effect of the Eucharist on each of our individual lives (that is, our transformation into Christ) will become lasting, because one of the conditions for this to happen is that we do his will, in which we find all the virtues and all that he desires of us. In the same way, the transformation of all of us collectively into the Church, which is another effect of the Eucharist, will also become lasting, because of the mutual love among us, which is the condition for our becoming the Church. We will love Jesus Forsaken, not wanting anything but him; and the Risen Jesus will always triumph in our midst, turning our lives into a continual Easter.

Yes, just as Archbishop Runcie, the Primate of the Anglican Church, reminded us recently: we of the Work of Mary want to be *an Easter people*. And if we love Jesus Forsaken, that is what we will be. Through our Holy Journey we will draw a great number of people to God, people who will be convinced that Christ is risen, because they will have discovered him risen in our midst.

Rocca di Papa, April 15, 1982

A SEVEN-FACET DIAMOND

The Priests and Religious Day,[9] with all its solemnity, is over. Let's hope that it has given great glory to God and also to the Church. But what will remain of that day will be, above all, the extent to which each one of us travelled forward on the Holy Journey during those hours. It shouldn't be any different for us today, than it was then, on April 30. Today too we must go forward toward our goal, guided by the Word of Life.

The Word of Life for May is this: "You are clean already, thanks to the word I have spoken to you" (Jn. 15:3). What words has Jesus spoken to us? We know that the two pillars of the Focolare are unity and Jesus Forsaken. Unity is the fruit of love for Jesus Forsaken: if we love him, we also have unity.

During this month dedicated to Mary, we want to offer her our efforts to embrace everything which represents Jesus Forsaken. We want to love him, we want him to be our life. We want to love him in our neighbors, because every neighbor has been paid for by Jesus at the price of his abandonment. And we want to love him especially in our brothers and sisters who share our Ideal, so that with them we can be, as we say, a single "cluster."

Recently I have received from all over, not only all kinds of pictures, drawings, and sculptures depicting clusters, especially from the gens, but also articles, prayers, and fables which have to do with clusters. A religious who belongs to the Servants of Mary sent me, for example, a book describing the seven founders of his Order, whom he described as a "cluster of lives." I read this work with great interest, and noticed once again how works which draw their inspiration from the Blessed Mother are profoundly similar. These seven founders, who were lay people (and some of whom were married) — and for whose canonization Pope Leo XIII decreed that it was enough to have four miracles, obtained by invoking the seven of them collectively — became saints in unity, because they made mutual love and communitarian witness the reason for their lives, and they were nourished by a special love for the Blessed Mother. It has been written of them, that they were *"a seven-facet diamond"*; and even though all seven of them were saints, they did not found seven religious families, but one.

How I want to emulate them! Don't you feel your hearts burning with the desire to give today the same extraordinary example they gave? Don't you see how fortunate we are to still be alive and to have a marvelous communitarian spirituality, and to belong to a work of God that he has put together in such a way that with this spirituality, we can offer him and the world not just one cluster of lives, but a whole vine of clusters — even more, a vineyard extending throughout the world, that offers all nations and races, the inebriating wine of the love of God and neighbor? Aren't we, the Work of Mary, the vineyard of Jesus Forsaken?[10] It is nothing extraordinary, therefore, if we accomplish all these things.

The example of Radi,[11] who has gone to the Heavenly Mariapolis, gives us hope. Some of us feel that she had reached this kind of sanctity, as a result of the Holy Journey we are travelling on together; and this gives us courage and certainty. So forward then, without stopping, loving one another out of love for Jesus Forsaken, especially when, in loving, we feel something of his abandonment. Onward! And if we welcome his "word" to us, which is everything that represents him forsaken, then we will be "clean already."

"Clean." What does this mean? It means saintly, holy.

St. Therese of the Child Jesus used to pray in this way: "I have only this fleeting day to offer you, as the fruit of my love, this cluster, in which every grape is a soul. Give me the fire of an apostle, Jesus, and do it today!"[12]

Rocca di Papa, May 6, 1982

A FAITHFULNESS CONTEST

Here we are again at our bi-weekly appointment, whose purpose is to give all of us a hand in making our life a Holy Journey; that is, to help us spend the time we have left the best way we can, following the teachings of Jesus. It is still May, and the Word of Life which lights up our path is: "You are clean already, thanks to the word I have spoken to you" (Jn. 15:3). As you know, two weeks ago we saw that the "word" God has spoken to us, to the Focolare, is everything which we understand as Jesus Forsaken, it is to love Jesus Forsaken.

I think and hope that all of us have done as much as we could to live this way. I too have tried to make this the program of my life during these last two weeks, and once again I have seen clearly that Jesus Forsaken is our life. Every act of love for him gives a new thrust to our Journey. It is tonic for the soul. And we feel like saying that the Gospel is really right: "Whoever loses his life for my sake will save it" (Lk. 9:24). It is really by dying that we live. This is our experience every day, every hour.

When we don't live this way; when we don't say no to our ego by denying ourselves and leaping out of our will into God's will, like kangaroos[13], as it were; when we don't mortify our ego, to make ourselves one with our neighbor, then we have the impression that we are not living, but— how should I put it? —vegetating. And so, during these final days of May, let's perfect our love for Jesus Forsaken.

Something which never ceases to amaze me, and which moves me when I see it in our lives, is the faithfulness of Jesus Forsaken. He has made himself so one with everyone, to such a sublime and heroic degree, by being the first to practice this art of loving, that every person on earth can feel he is close to them in every difficulty, and especially in moments of suffering.

Do we feel forsaken or alone? He is there. Betrayed or humiliated? He is there, too. Do we feel lukewarm, disoriented, excluded? Failures or sinners? He is there. He is always faithful. He never fails to be there. In fact, just when everybody else disappears, that is the moment when he appears.

Well then, let this be our resolution for the next two weeks: *to compete with his faithfulness*, to be wherever he is, unwavering, ready to love him, to embrace him.

Is he there in some personal sufferings we have? Then let's be there with him. Is he in our family, which is suffering, in our community, which is lacking the sunshine of love, of unity? Let's be there. Is he in the divisions among Christians? Let's be there in the front lines! Is he in those who do not know the true faith? Let's be there too. Is he in our cold, atheistic, or secularistic environment? Let's be there too, to embrace him in that coldness.

Yes, for these next two weeks, let's compete with him, with his faithfulness. In this way we will make him happy, and he will say to us: "You are already clean because of the word I have spoken to you." And if we are already clean (which—as we know—means holy), then we can be sure that we are truly on a Holy Journey.

Rocca di Papa, May 20, 1982

LET'S MAKE LIFE EASY FOR JESUS
IN OUR MIDST

Since I spent last week at Loppiano,[14] I just had to spend a few hours visiting the Shrine at Monte Senario, the burial place of the Seven Holy Founders, who in the thirteenth century reached the goal of sanctity all together. Standing there before their precious relics, after having prayed to Jesus and Mary, whom they had loved so much, I asked these seven to be the special protectors of this bi-weekly conference call, which we are using to help one another reach sanctity together. After I finished this brief prayer, I then admired a fresco painted on one of the walls of the little church, which depicts a miracle in the lives of those saints. It was the middle of winter, and a grapevine began to sprout leaves, to blossom, and to produce tasty bunches of grapes. They interpreted this extraordinary fact as a sign that it was God's will that they welcome many other members into their religious family.

Naturally, as you can understand, this happy coincidence between the Seven Holy Founders and the vine with the clusters of grapes (a symbol for us of the way we want to be "organized") made me happy; and I felt more strongly than ever the desire to make the mystical vineyard of Jesus Forsaken blossom in the winter of this world, which has been made so cold by materialism.

We are at the beginning of a new month, whose Word of Life is a special one for us, since we have centered our attention this year on the Risen Lord: "And know that I am with you always, until the end of the world" (Mt. 28:20). Jesus has promised to be with us always. Therefore he will be with us during these next two weeks as well, because he wants to be in our company.

What should our response to this be? With infinite gratitude for this decision of his, we should prepare ourselves the best we can to be with him. If we knew that some important person had decided to come and stay at our house for a few days, we would certainly make sure that the door was open when he got there. We would prepare for his visit, arranging everything with him in mind.

Now, we know that Jesus himself is with us every day, until the end of the world. What should we do then? I think it's a good idea, first of all, to know where we can find him. We know that he is present in the Eucharist, in the poor, in those who act and speak in his name, in his word, and in each one of us, through grace.

But this year we members of the Focolare have come to understand that he wants us to find him in one place in particular: in our midst. This is his desire. In fact, one of his goals when he brought the Focolare to life was to be able to be present everywhere, not only within church walls, but wherever people are.

So during these next two weeks, let's make room for Jesus in our midst, especially in our clusters. From there, he can radiate love and light to many other people in the world around us. By calling to mind our duty to serve others, and making ourselves one with one another, we will make it possible for him to live in our midst, we will make it easy for him. So, may he reign among us! May he remain with us, so that, for these two weeks at least, we can be with him. We couldn't ask for a better friend on our Journey; and we cannot measure the effects of his divine companionship.

Here then is a very useful motto for the next two weeks: *Let's make life easy for Jesus in our midst.*

Rocca di Papa, June 3, 1982

JESUS FORSAKEN AND THE TWELVE STARS
OF PERFECTION

The goal of this bi-weekly appointment is to strengthen our unity and to encourage us to go toward sanctity together. This time, I would like to tell you about a very recent spiritual experience I had. As you probably know, I decided to spend several days this month examining in depth a part of our spirituality which will be the focus of formation for the members of the Focolare this coming year: Jesus Forsaken, the key to unity.

It touched me so deeply, and I found it so interesting and appealing, that I tried to center my whole life on it immediately, in the present moment; almost forgetting my commitment to strive for sanctity. So I've been trying to love Jesus Forsaken, embracing him in whatever guise he presented himself. But just a few days ago, during my morning meditation, I again came across St. John of the Cross's Twelve Stars of Perfection[15]. That is: love of God, love of neighbor, chastity, poverty, obedience, peace, silence, humility, mortification, penance, prayer in choir, and private prayer. I knew them well. In fact, I had meditated on them so much, that I knew them by heart. But lately I hadn't thought of them at all; I was so taken up by loving Jesus Forsaken.

Then came the surprise, a joyful surprise, a kind of luminous rediscovery. Reading again about those Twelve Stars during my meditation, I realized that by loving Jesus Forsaken, I had made all of them shine a little brighter in my soul. I had loved God a little more, because I had loved Jesus Forsaken, who is God. I had loved my neighbor more, because for love of Jesus Forsaken I had made an effort to make myself one with everyone. I had increased chastity, because love for Jesus Forsaken leads us to mortify ourselves. And the same with poverty, because for him I had tried to extinguish every attachment. I had improved in obedience, because for him I had made an effort to silence my own self in order to listen better to the "inner voice"[16]. By loving Jesus Forsaken in suffering I had remained at peace. Loving him, I had observed silence better, holding back useless words. Humility had also increased with this dying to myself which love for Jesus Forsaken produces. The same with mortification and penance. I had improved "prayer in choir," which for me means prayer in common with the other *focolarini*. And my personal prayer was more meaningful also. So everything improved, just because of love for Jesus Forsaken. I knew that he was, as we say, a monument of holiness, but I hadn't yet experienced so clearly that to love Jesus Forsaken is really a most fruitful way to strive for sanctity.

I cannot wish you anything better than to have this experience yourselves. Try it! Love Jesus Forsaken in every suffering, in every act of self-denial, and, above all, in dying to yourself to "make yourself one" with every neighbor, so as to be in harmony with this month's Word of Life, which speaks of the presence of the Risen Lord in our midst. May Jesus Forsaken become everything for us! Then our collective sanctity will be assured.

Rocca di Papa, June 16, 1982

THE MOTIVATING FORCE OF
OUR EVERY ACTION

I am really grateful to God because I see that love for Jesus Forsaken during the month of July has made the Twelve Stars of Perfection shine a little brighter in many of us.

August's Word of Life is: "Nothing that goes into a man from outside can make him unclean; it is the things that come out of a man that make him unclean" (Mk. 7:15 JB). It confronts us, as we have read in the commentary, with the necessity of being ready to love God and our neighbor at every moment. Only if we have this attitude, can we be sure that what comes out of our innermost being (thoughts, desires, hopes, deeds, and so on) is good, worthy of persons who see life as a Holy Journey.

In these first few days of August, I, like you, have also tried to put this new Word into practice, because it was God's will, and because I wanted to share my experience with you and encourage us all to go forward. And I have noticed that at the examination of conscience in the evening, if I have anything to be sorry about, it is always something that has not been the fruit of love, that has not been rooted in love. And the same is probably true for all of you. It is not—we hope—the theft, murder, adultery, wickedness, fraud, and so on, that Jesus enumerates, that obscure our life as committed Christians, but rather small vanities, attachments, judgments, resentments, selfishness, surges of pride, distractions during prayer, envy, haste, lack of commitment, sins of gluttony—all defects that jeopardize the Holy Journey. So what should we do?

The watchword is: Love! Love God and neighbor! How? With all our heart, not saving even a bit for something else. In every moment of the day, let's be able to say: "Yes, Jesus, in this moment, in this deed, I loved you with my whole heart." And let's do it not so much to be perfect, but because we love him.

So let's start! Let's make sure that *the motivating force of our every action* is love. Then, in the evening we will find nothing to be sorry about; rather, our heart will be full of gratitude toward God.

Sierre, August 5, 1982

LOVE SO GREAT THAT WE RISK
OUR LIVES

We left each other two weeks ago with the desire to root our Christian life each present moment in love, to make love the motivating force of our every action. This seemed the best way to live the Word of Life: "Nothing that goes into a man from outside can make him unclean...." (Mk. 7:15 JB).

What experience can I share with you that would give us a hand in this Holy Journey?

Trying to love God and my neighbor, I have understood that we Christians are truly ourselves if we love; that is, if we don't think about ourselves, but about God, about his will, which is above all to love our neighbor. God asks this of us: if we want to *be*, to be truly ourselves, to be fulfilled as Christians, we must *not be*, we must live "outside" ourselves, living not our will but God's, "living" our neighbor. Then we are truly ourselves.

I have tried to live this way—to love. But I have realized that there are various degrees of love. I have seen that just having a certain amount of understanding for others, taking an interest in their sufferings, trying somehow to carry their burdens with them—in other words, having a love which is kind of so-so, is not enough, if we are to be the way Jesus wants us to be. God demands that we love, and that we show our love with acts that reflect—at least in our intention—the measure of his love for us: "Love one another *as I have loved you*" (Jn. 15:12).

Therefore we must always be ready to die for our neighbor, and whatever we do, moment by moment, to show our love concretely, must be animated and sustained by this desire, this decision. This is the only sort of love that is pleasing to Jesus — not just any sort of love, or a coating of love, but *love so great that we risk our lives.*

Loving this way, we live completely "outside" ourselves. We dethrone our ego. And if there are more than one of us doing this, then we can really hope that we are "abdicating" in favor of the Risen Lord, who will thus be able to reign among us. For, in fact, he is fully present not where there is just a little love, but where there are people united in his name; that is, in him, according to his will, which is to love as he has loved us.

And so every time we meet neighbors during these next two weeks, whether we are talking to them over the phone or writing them a letter, whether we are preparing a talk for them or carrying out our daily work in their service, let us always ask ourselves: "Am I ready to die for them?"

If we do this, I am certain that during these next two weeks, our life of love will take a step forward, a big step forward in quality. So then, ten, twenty times a day, whenever we do something for our neighbor, let's ask ourselves: "Am I ready to give my life for her? Am I ready to give my life for him?"

Sierre, August 19, 1982

For a year now, all of us in the Focolare all over the world have been trying to deepen our understanding of what it means to live with the Risen Lord in our midst. September invites us to live according to a new Word of Life, which is radical and emphatic, leaving no room for doubt: "If your foot should cause you to sin, cut it off; it is better for you to enter into life lame, than to have two feet and be thrown into hell" (Mk. 9:45 JB). With these words, Jesus is certainly not telling us to mutilate our bodies; rather, by using such an expression, he wants to show us how demanding his moral stance is: When we are faced with circumstances which could cause us to fall into evil, we must start "cutting," and cut decisively.

If up to now, we have tried to chase away the temptations to evil that came to us from the world, the flesh, and the devil, this month our reaction must be even quicker and more decisive. We must "cut" immediately, without mercy. But for us, who want to continue this Holy Journey our whole life, it is not enough to avoid evil. We must also do good.

What good must we do? The good that God's will wants from us in the present moment. And since we are still focusing on what it means to live with the Risen Lord in our midst, we must do our best to live for unity, "making ourselves one" with every neighbor, "cutting" away anything that could interfere with this.

Many factors can jeopardize our having this attitude of love: at times, distractions; at other times, the mistaken desire to hastily express our ideas or to give advice at the wrong time. Sometimes we lack the readiness to "make ourselves one" with our neighbors because we think that they will misinterpret our love. In other instances, we are prevented from loving because we judge them, or because we have a hidden desire to win them over to our side. At times we are incapable of "making ourselves one" because our heart is filled with our own worries, sufferings, interests, and plans.

So how can we "make ourselves one" and take upon ourselves our neighbor's concerns, sufferings, and anxieties? By "cutting" and setting aside everything which fills our mind and our heart.

So then, to end this year well, at least like the workers of the last hour, let us remember these few words: "cut," so we can be freer, more total in our love; "cut," *so we can love better.*

If we are committed to living like this all day long, not only will we do the good things we do better, but we will also avoid evil; because whoever makes himself one is loving, and whoever loves does not sin.

Forward then! *Let's "cut," so we can love better.*

Solingen, September 2, 1982

YES TO JESUS; NO TO OUR EGO

These first two weeks of September we tried to "cut," so we could love better and put the Word of Life into practice: "If your foot should cause you to sin, cut it off ...." (Mk. 9:45 JB). We now have two more weeks to go more deeply into this Word of Life, so as to live out our specific vocation more fully; that is, to live in unity, to let the Risen Lord live in our midst.

A few days ago, I read a wonderful passage from the letters of St. Paul, and it made me understand how he personally lived those "cuts" that Jesus speaks about. After encouraging the Christians to imitate athletes, who undergo a lot of sacrifices to win the wreath of victory, he speaks of himself and says: "What I do is discipline my own body and master it, for fear that after having preached to others I myself should be rejected" (1 Cor. 9:27).

In fact, Paul had to look after a "cluster" that had been entrusted to him; and it was not just one cluster, but many vines filled with clusters scattered in all the places he had evangelized. And as he thought of all those people, he felt the desire, the urge, the need to be an example for them. And that is why he says, "I discipline my body and make it my slave." That is what we too must do with ourselves.

Is our ego rebelling against God's will, not wanting to work as it should, to study properly, to pray attentively, to accept burdensome situations lovingly, even when they are painful? Does it want to free itself of the obligation to love each neighbor? Does it want to speak ill of someone, to be impatient, to judge, to get even, at least a little? Then this

65

is the moment to discipline ourself, to say no to ourself, and to show no mercy. No! No! No! Ten, twenty, thirty times a day!

But we know there's a way that's typically ours, a way to say no not only ten or twenty times a day, but continuously, all day long. And that way is to say yes to Jesus, to his will; to say yes to our neighbors, in everything except sin; to always say yes—always, with all our heart. These yeses to Jesus are a solemn no to our own ego. With these yeses to Jesus, we don't leave any room for our own self, we master it. These yeses to Jesus sound the death knell for our ego.

So during these next two weeks, let's always say yes to Jesus in the present moment; and if something within us rebels, let's master it with a decisive no!

Yes to Jesus; no to our ego.

Sierre, September 16, 1982

66

CONCRETE SERVICE

As we all know, the stupendous, divine, formidable theme for this year, our reason for living, the goal we are constantly striving for, is unity—the Risen Lord in our midst. However, examining the aims of the Focolare more closely, we see that to have the presence of the Risen Lord among its members is not a one-year commitment, but its goal in every time, in every place.

In fact, although the specific goal of the Focolare is to work in every possible way for the realization of the Testament of Jesus, "That all may be one" (Jn. 17:21), the general aim is the perfection of love—to be "perfect in love." And we are perfect in love when we have the Risen Lord in our midst. In fact, I have always been struck by that phrase of St. John the evangelist, which says: "If we love one another, God dwells in us, and his love is brought to perfection in us" (1 Jn. 4:12). The love of God in us is perfect if we love one another. But if we love one another, the Risen Lord is in our midst. In unity with him we are perfect, and therefore, we are holy. We can then be certain that our life is a Holy Journey. Let us always live in such a way that the Risen Lord will shine forth from our midst.

The new Word of Life for October can help us in this. It says: "Whoever wants to rank first among you must serve the needs of all" (Mk. 10:43). We must serve our neighbor, serve every neighbor. How? The way Jesus wants. He was thinking of concrete, practical acts of service, such as his washing the feet of his disciples. We could actually view our whole life as an act of service, whether we work for the good of society or for the good of the Church.

The new Word of Life urges us to fill our day with humble and intelligent acts of service, to do whatever is asked of us to make ourselves one with every neighbor we meet during the day: to set the table; straighten up the house; do the shopping; care for the sick; to instruct, comfort, or console; to give something which is ours; to admonish with love, and so on. And we know that if we make ourselves one with others, sooner or later this love will become mutual, and then the Risen Lord will be in our midst.

The Word of Life really helps us to bring about unity, which is our goal—not just this year but always—because we of the Work of Mary are called to give life to Christ in the midst of the world, just like Mary, our Mother. And so this month let's aim at serving others. Let our watchword be: *"concrete service."*

Rocca di Papa, October 7, 1982

READY TO DIE FOR OUR NEIGHBOR,
LIKE ST. MAXIMILIAN KOLBE

There is still a festive atmosphere here in Rome, following the canonization of Father Maximilian Kolbe. The newspapers wrote about it, the television showed films about him, and biographies of him, both old and new, are in all the bookstores. And we too have been caught up in this atmosphere.

But what most impressed me when I read one of his biographies, was the fact that this new saint is very close to us, because of his passionate love for the Blessed Mother, and also because he loved with the measure of Jesus' love, to the point of giving his life. Face-to-face with a prisoner, a person unknown to him, destined to die of hunger in the death bunker, but who was his neighbor in that moment, Kolbe took his place, forgetting at once all the great work he was doing for the Kingdom of God—his vast editorial activity, his little cities of the Immaculate, his spiritual children, his workload of papers (There was a picture of him at his desk piled high with work).

Couldn't Father Kolbe have thought, that with the work he had begun in the Church, he would have been able to glorify God more by staying alive than by dying? Instead, he didn't hesitate to offer his life to save the father of a family.

We, too, during the course of the day, frequently carry out jobs that are important, at least in our eyes. And sometimes, while we are busy doing these things, we are "disturbed"—as we would put it—by neighbors who intrude unexpectedly, in person, over the phone, through a letter, or in some other way, asking us to do something. In those moments, filled with the importance we think our work has, we do not even give these persons a glance, we don't pay attention to their request, we put them off, we even treat them badly.

Here Father Kolbe gives us a solemn lesson. This is not the way to love our neighbor; this is not the way to serve. With each person, we must know how to forget everything we are doing, whether it's beautiful, great, or useful—even if it may only be for a few moments, if our duty calls us to something else. We must be ready to "make ourselves one" with our neighbor in everything, to "make ourselves one" with the measure of one who is ready to die for the other person. This is the Christian life.

How then should we live this Word of Life which speaks to us of service? By making the decision to be ready to die for all those for whom we carry out our daily work, and in particular those neighbors who come upon us unexpectedly. Let us repeat in our hearts: *I am ready to die for my neighbor, like St. Maximilian Kolbe.*

Rocca di Papa, October 21, 1982

LET'S "MAKE OURSELVES ONE"
WITH HIM

For the past few months of our Holy Journey, we have tried to increase our love for our neighbor, particularly by making ourselves one with everyone; so that if love became mutual, the Risen Lord might be able to live in our midst. This has undoubtedly deepened our relationship with God, for we know that love of neighbor and love of God increase one another reciprocally.

During November, instead, we have a Word of Life that stresses faith — faith in God who is all powerful, the kind of faith which obtains favors: "Be on your way. Your faith has healed you " (Mk. 10:52).

What is the best way to put this into practice? If you have read the commentary, you have seen that the faith which wells up in our hearts and is a necessary condition for God to work, is only the first step toward what he wants from us. This trust in him is the beginning of a relationship which must develop and become a deep communion.

So the best thing for us to do, if we want to properly interpret Jesus' will as he expresses it in this Word of Life, is to cultivate our union with God, to seek a deeper union with him. If we do this, then we will certainly be seeking the kingdom of God, and everything else will come to us as a consequence. By trying to be deeply united with God, we will truly be seeking his kingdom, and all our problems will find their solutions. The favors we desire and ask for with love, we will obtain.

Therefore, let's seek union with God. The gens talk about "going deeper." So let's keep "going deeper" in our union with God all day long, by doing his will. But during this month let's focus particularly on the moments during the day when we express our union with God. Let those wonderful prayers which we recite each morning and evening, or when we go to visit Jesus in the tabernacle, truly come from our hearts. Let those words which we repeat so many times in the rosary, be truly ours, expressions of our love. Let's plunge into union with God during meditation, so that we can feel again that vigor which is ever new and which is released in our spirit when we read the Scriptures, or go deeper into our spirituality, or penetrate the thoughts of the saints. Let's plunge into union with God with at least as much enthusiasm as we had when making ourselves one with our neighbor these past months. *Let's "make ourselves one" with him,* silencing everything in us so that we might be able to hear his voice.

Then let's go to Mass and receive Holy Communion with all the love our hearts can muster. Let's be aware that in the Eucharist we have a gift to offer God which is worthy of him; which can say to him that we love him, that we adore him, that we praise him. Let's be convinced that in Jesus, who is being sacrificed on the altar, we have someone who can ask the Father's forgiveness for us, someone who can say thank you to the Father in a way that will be accepted, someone who can ask him for blessings and favors, and obtain them.

Let's be faithful in offering God those moments that are reserved for him, and live them perfectly, interiorly, and exteriorly. Yes, even the sign of the cross should be dignified, worthy of the One we are naming. When we genuflect, let's do it well. If those who do not know Jesus, but seek God, are so precise in doing these outward things, how much more should we be!

We should be at least as precise, doing everything perfectly, with that composure, dignity, and conviction that by themselves will radiate our faith. And if our communion with God becomes more perfect, then the whole rest of our day will soon begin to feel its beneficial effects. On our Holy Journey train,[17] we will ride higher and higher, closer and closer to him. And as our love increases, our faith will increase, too. We will do everything in agreement with him. We will entrust our anxieties to him, and we will hear him repeat: "Be on your way. Your faith has healed you."

Rocca di Papa, November 4, 1982

"Be on your way. Your faith has saved you." (Mk. 10:52). This is the Word of Life we are studying and trying to live this month. How important faith is for Jesus! In our spirituality we usually stress love more. And this is right: perfection in love, in fact, is the first purpose of our life. This is our vocation, but do we think enough about how indispensable faith is to reaching the goal for which God brought about the Focolare?

We try to become perfect in love by perfecting our love day by day, hour by hour; and we have almost reached the 700th day of our Holy Journey. All of us, more or less, according to how generous we are, make daily efforts to keep going, and if we have fallen behind in the race, to pick ourselves up and catch up. But perhaps, even though we know that without God's grace we cannot get anywhere, we still live our thrust towards sanctity by giving too much weight to our own efforts, as if it were all our own business, as if it were all a matter of will power. And in spite of our daily efforts, we find that we are still loaded down with defects. We observe, when we examine ourselves, that the result we have achieved is not at all in proportion to the effort expended, and it is not in proportion, especially, to the long period of time we have been involved in this Holy Journey—more than a hundred and twenty weeks!

Well, what should we do then? We have a Word of Life this month in which Jesus offers us a fabulous remedy to save us, as he says, not only from our physical ills, but from our moral ills: the bad habits, defects, attachments, weaknesses, and vices that we still have. The remedy for all of this is our faith.

"Be on your way. Your faith has saved you." This is the hour, this is the moment, in which we should not let this promising invitation of Jesus pass us by. This is the opportunity to take serious steps forward. This is the hour to revitalize our faith.

During these final days of November, it would be a very good idea to make this the purpose of our prayer, beginning with Mass and Holy Communion—asking God to give us the grace to be perfect, perfect in love. Let's ask for this grace with faith, with burning faith, faith which has been revitalized by the conviction that we are not asking anything other than what he wants from us. And he will surely give it to us, if he is certain that our confidence rests in him and not in ourselves.

So then, we are all in agreement: *Great faith so we can love better.* This is our motto.

Rocca di Papa, November 18, 1982

TO GOD THROUGH OUR NEIGHBOR

The Word of Life that should be a light for our Holy Journey this month is: "Make ready the way of the Lord, clear him a straight path" (Lk. 3:4). The fact is that the Lord is about to come. Christmas is getting closer and the liturgy invites us to prepare the way for him. Jesus entered into history two thousand years ago. Now he wants to enter our life, but the way into us is full of obstacles. We must flatten the little mountains, remove the rocks.

What are these obstacles that can block the way for Jesus? They are all the desires which arise in our souls that are not in conformity with God's will. They are the attachments we still cling to. These include the desire to speak or to be quiet when we ought to do otherwise, the desire to affirm ourselves, the desire for esteem, for perfection, for material things, for health, or for life itself, when these are not God's will. Then there are worse desires: to rebel, to judge, to get revenge. When such desires arise in our souls, they seem to take over.

We must extinguish these desires, take away these obstacles, get down to doing God's will, and thus prepare the way for the Lord. The Word of Life says to make his paths straight. Make them straight; that's exactly what we must do. These desires lead us astray. By extinguishing them, we put ourselves back on the right track, in the ray of God's will.

But there is a way which is typically ours, which we can be sure will keep us on the straight path and lead us for certain to God, our goal. This way obliges us to pass through our neighbor.

This month let's throw ourselves again into loving every neighbor we meet during the day. Let's enkindle in our hearts that ardent and praiseworthy desire that God certainly wants us to have: the desire to love every neighbor by "making ourselves one" with them in everything, unselfishly and without limits.

Let's have this attitude especially towards those people who are part of our cluster, in the great vineyard of Jesus Forsaken, which is the Work of Mary. Love will give new life to people and to relationships, and will prevent selfish desires from arising. In fact, love is the best antidote for such desires. In this way we will be able to prepare a gift for Jesus, when he comes at Christmas. The gift will be our abundant fruit, and our heart which has been burned up and consumed in love.

The motto which can remind us of this resolution is: *To God through our neighbor.*

Rocca di Papa, December 2, 1982

TO BE WHAT WE ACTUALLY ARE,
LET'S BE LOVE

It's still December, the month of Advent. Christmas is just around the corner. The Word of Life repeats: "Make ready the way of the Lord, clear him a straight path" (Lk. 3:4).

Two weeks ago we spoke about the obstacles we had to eliminate, the little mountains in our life that had to be levelled. And in regard to these little mountains, I would like to share with you today the wonderful impression I had when I read the following words of St. Paul: "Get rid of the old yeast, and make yourselves into a completely new batch of bread, unleavened as you are meant to be" (1 Cor. 5:7 JB).

What does leaven do? It swells things up. Think of crackers which are filled with all those air bubbles due to leaven. For St. Paul, leaven in this context is a symbol for evil. Evil, in fact, seems to satisfy our desires or "appetites," as John of the Cross would say. It seems to fill our soul, but that's actually only an illusion. Paul invites us to get rid of this kind of swelling. He says, "You are meant to be unleavened," that is, without yeast.

We might ask ourselves why Paul says that we must get rid of the old yeast, while at the same time he affirms that we are already unleavened? Here we have Paul's whole moral teaching summed up: We are already Christians through grace. We are already love (grace is God's love in us). We are already pure (grace has purified us; in fact, it has "divinized" us), but we have to *be* what we actually are. We have to correspond to this grace. Christianity involves both God's mysterious action and our constant effort to correspond.

This passage struck me so much, because I see the whole of our spirituality summed up in it. We want nothing, but to be that what we actually are: to be true Christians individually, and to be the body of Christ collectively. This is what the Holy Spirit has been urging us to do through our spirituality: *to be what we actually are.*

So then, as we await Christmas, let's try to truly be what we are: to be love, loving God first of all, by being his will in each present moment, and loving everyone so that we can have Jesus in our midst constantly. This is the most beautiful homage we can offer to the Child Jesus on his birthday; and to his Mother, Mary, whom we "relive" by living in this way.

Everything is contained in love. It is love that overcomes the leaven of evil in us. It is love which prepares the way for the One who is coming. So during these days let's not forget to be what we really are. This could be our motto: *To be what we actually are, let's be love.*

Rocca di Papa, December 16, 1982

1983

THE EXTRAORDINARY OPPORTUNITY
WE CANNOT PASS UP

1982 has ended, 1983 has begun. These are days for balancing accounts and making resolutions, for drawing the balance after two years of the Holy Journey and resolving to go all the way to the end; that is, to the day when we can offer Mary the gift of our sanctity.[18]

Recently, looking at the little calendar which reminds us each day of our loved ones who have reached the Heavenly Mariapolis (as we refer to our brothers and sisters who are no longer with us on earth), I noticed that there isn't a great difference between the number of children and youth (the gen 3's and the gen 2's) in the Heavenly Mariapolis, and the number of older people (the volunteers, *focolarini*, and priests). In all probability, this year, too, some of us will go to the Heavenly Mariapolis; and it is not a bad idea for each of us to stop and consider for a moment, that it might be our turn. Sooner or later the moment comes for everyone. And looking at things in this perspective, we cannot help seeing the life we have left (whether months or years) as a great opportunity, a unique opportunity, one we should not let slip by, an opportunity to achieve something truly great, beautiful and holy. But how?

January's Word of Life invites us to reflect on what Jesus said of himself: "I am the life" (Jn. 14:6). He was speaking of the supernatural life he came on earth to share with us, the extraordinary life that does not die, that lasts forever. With that life we can transform our earthly life into something wonderful, divine, and great; and we can contribute to the fulfillment of God's plan for humanity, and produce extraordinary, everlasting fruits. To take the greatest advantage of the life we still have, we should join our life to this superior Life, which is Jesus himself.

The commentary on the Word of Life points out three sources we can draw from to accomplish this. The first of these is faith, which is the adherence of our hearts to Christ. The second is the Eucharist. The third is Jesus' words when we put them into practice.

I think that we who listen to this conference call already have faith and that all of us, more or less frequently, nourish ourselves on the Eucharist. In one way or another, therefore, we are already taking advantage of these two sources. What we have to do now is to put all our effort and strength into living according to his words.

Which words? The Words of Life offered to us each month. During the next two weeks let's make every effort to put the words which are the basis of the Focolare life and the synthesis of Christianity into practice: let's love one another as Jesus has loved us. He loved us to the point of experiencing abandonment. Let's love every person we meet in the same way.

So that we won't miss out on this great chance we are being given in the time we still have, let's take advantage of every opportunity we have to love one another with the measure of his love; that is, with total emptiness of self, "making ourselves completely one" with everyone, so that the Risen Lord may be present in our midst. Let's offer the Risen Lord to the world; let's give life to Jesus as Mary did. This is *the extraordinary opportunity we cannot pass up.*

Sierre, January 4, 1983

"I am the life" (Jn. 14:6), is what Jesus continues to repeat to us during this second half of January. And "I am *your* life," is what he is saying softly to each one of us.

"I am *your* life, gen"; "I am *your* life, *focolarino*, or priest, volunteer, religious, or other member of the Focolare." Yes, because through God's grace and our response to it, his life flourishes in our hearts. In fact, by loving God and our neighbor, we have allowed our love to develop. We have given our supernatural personality the chance to express itself. We have allowed Jesus to live in us. His life is in us, and this is the most precious thing we possess, the most precious thing that every consistent Christian possesses.

We can perceive this Life in some way with the senses of the soul. When, for example, after having faithfully loved our neighbor all day, we turn inward to pray, Jesus is there present. We can sense him there welcoming us, waiting to listen to us.

The Work of Mary is, as we know, the vineyard of Jesus Forsaken. And each of us individually is a vine, a vine alive with the Life that is Jesus, who said, "I am the life."

I am always impressed, especially during the winter, when I see how the grapevines are cultivated here in Valais, Switzerland. How much care is given to them, and what discipline they are subjected to! They give excellent wine, that's true, but how much work they demand! You see them lined up in perfectly straight rows, equidistant from one another, so that each one will be fully exposed to the sun. You see how they are perfectly pruned of all the useless branches, so that in some instances only one branch is left to bear its abundant fruit, its succulent bunches of grapes. They are tied firmly to a stick so that they will stand straight and not drag on the ground. All the ground around them is cleaned of the many leaves that fell during the harvest. If the vines are still very small, you see them surrounded by a circular net to protect them; and so on, with still other clever devices.

I thought of us, of the little vine, of Jesus' life growing in us, and of the care which we should give it. We must first of all keep it in the sunlight, well-exposed to God's presence in prayer, when we converse with Jesus in our heart. We must keep it well-pruned of all the useless branches; that is, of all the activities that we would like to engage in, but which are not God's will for us. We must keep this life firmly bound to Jesus Forsaken, who enables us to love the suffering which comes upon us unexpectedly, as well as the suffering which self-denial involves. We must maintain the ground around our vine clean, keeping far away from us the things or persons that were a cause of temptation in our past life: unhealthy friendships, various little vices, television programs that it would be better not to watch, useless objects, and other vain things. And above all, if our grapevine is still small, we must protect it with our unity with those who share our spirituality—in the life of the Focolare household, of the volunteer nucleus, of the gen unit, or of the Focolare community.

We must spend the rest of our life cultivating Jesus' life in us, so that the immense vineyard of Jesus Forsaken may grow and develop more and more throughout the world, until the moment when all will be one.

But since each day has moments of prayer, of self-denial, of suffering to be embraced; and since temptations, old loves or attachments which must be overcome may return; and since there are also moments for getting together in the Focolare house or with the Focolare community, then to do all that I have said before to cultivate our beloved vine, it is enough to plunge ourselves one hundred percent into whatever God wants from us in each present moment and to repeat in our heart the words of Pope John XXIII: "I must do everything ... as if I had nothing else to do, as if the Lord had put me in this world for the sole purpose of doing that thing well...."[19]

This is the way then: *Be totally absorbed in whatever God wants from us in the present moment, as if we had nothing else to do, as if we had been born for that alone.*

Sierre, January 20, 1983

"Whoever does not go forward, goes backwards." This is what St. Bernard and various Fathers of the Church say regarding the interior life and progress toward sanctity, or as we would put it, the Holy Journey. "Whoever does not go forward," that is, whoever does not improve, doesn't stay still, but goes backwards. This is why we really need to be like mountain climbers who are roped together, helping and encouraging one another to keep taking little steps forward, thus avoiding the risk of sliding backwards.

The Word of Life comes to our aid in this. It is, as we know, a "lamp unto our feet." This month it says, "If you say so, I will lower the nets" (Lk. 5:5). This was Peter's reply when Jesus invited him to fish. It was certainly not the favorable moment to fish; quite the contrary. There was no human reason for Peter, therefore, to accept Jesus' invitation. But since he accepted his Master's invitation with faith, he had a miraculous catch.

We too are called to have an extraordinary catch, to be fishermen, not of fish, but of people—many people. We are called to work so "that all may be one." How can we bring about this catch? Peter says, "If you say so"; therefore, the means, the cause, the secret of the miraculous catch is to believe in what Jesus says, to believe in his word and to act upon it. His word, which is a "light for our path" and a guarantee that we will not go backwards but forwards, will also be the cause of our miraculous catch. We must really base our life on his word, constantly remaining faithful to it.

But which of Jesus' words should we focus our lives on, to which should we adhere? All of them, of course, and that is what we try to do month after month. This month, in which we have a choice, we will focus on Jesus himself as the Word of God, or better still, on Jesus Crucified and Forsaken whom we have always regarded as the Word completely revealed. Let's be close to him, therefore, during these next two weeks. Let's stay with him all day long, or better yet, let's say to him in each present moment: "I am *with you*."

If we do this, he will suggest the acts of virtue we should perform, the "cuts" we should make, the acts of mortification we should practice so that we may die to ourselves in every present moment and rise again to live in his will. Jesus Forsaken will enlighten us (since our way to God is through our neighbor) on how to be empty of ourselves so that we can make ourselves one with each person and he can win them to his heart. He will do a perfect job of teaching us what we call "the technique of unity," which is our way of giving our contribution so "that all may be one." And we will see the miraculous catch repeated in our lives.

With him, therefore, is the motto which summarizes our commitment for the present moments of the next two weeks. We are *with you*, Jesus Crucified and Forsaken, to keep going forward, because "Whoever does not go forward, goes backwards."

"With you!"

Rocca di Papa, February 3, 1983

We are still on our Journey. Time does not stand still, and neither should we. Our goal is getting closer. For more than two years now, we have been making every effort to go forward on our Holy Journey. But what results have there been, what progress have we made?

Perhaps, at times, not all the results have been positive. After having set out enthusiastically, our zeal may have diminished, tiredness may have set in. Or perhaps we are waiting for something to happen that will give us new vigor to take up the race again. When we are at a standstill like this, feeling a little uncertain, then things like our family, business, even the work we do at the service of the Work of Mary can totally absorb us. And so, as a result, we no longer feel that union with God, that splendid, unmistakable union with Him which in times past has been a wellspring of unparalled sweetness for us, a source of superhuman strength.

What can we do about it?

Even in this predicament, the Word of Life can help us. This month it continues to tell us: "If you say so, I will lower the nets" (Lk. 5:5). To let Peter experience the power of God, Jesus asked him for faith. He asked Peter to believe in him, to believe in something that was, humanly speaking, impossible, even absurd: to go fishing in the daytime, when the night had already been so fruitless.

If we want to return to life, if we want to have a miraculous catch of happiness, we too must believe; and we must, if necessary, face the risk of the absurd, which Jesus' words sometimes demand. We know that God's word is life, but we come into this life by passing through death. It is gain, but we gain by losing. It is growth, but we grow by diminishing. So, how can we arise from this state of spiritual tiredness into which we might have fallen? We can do it by accepting the risk of his word.

Frequently, influenced by the mentality of the world in which we live, we actually begin to believe that happiness lies in possessing things or in having other people think that we are important, in giving ourselves over to amusements or in dominating other people, in being in the limelight or satisfying our senses with eating and drinking. But none of these things are true.

So let's take the risk, and try breaking with all these things. Let's run the risk of dying completely. Let's risk! Let's risk! — Once, twice, ten times a day!

Then, in the evening, we will feel the sweetness of his love blossoming again in our heart. We will find again that union with him which we no longer hoped for. The light of his unmistakable inspirations will shine for us again. We will be filled with his consolation and peace, and we will feel protected by God our Father's loving gaze. And surrounded by his protection, we will once again feel strength, hope, confidence; the certainty that the Holy Journey is possible, and that this slowing down or stopping of ours was just a pause and nothing more. We will feel certain that the world can belong to him.

But it is necessary to risk death, nothingness, detachment. This is the price! Take courage then! Let the motto for these next two weeks be: *Risk at his word, to have a miraculous catch of happiness and of hearts that will love him.*

Rocca di Papa, February 17, 1983

91

I really hope that we are all journeying forward. And if someone has paused, I hope that he or she has gotten over it and has understood that, on this earth, the basic attitude to have is to be always ready to start over again, grateful to God for still giving us time to do it.

Forward then on our Holy Journey! It is vitally important—for us and for many others. In fact, because of the Communion of Saints, which binds us all together, whoever is "up"—as we say—striving to love, is keeping many others "up," who without him or her would have perhaps allowed themselves to be pulled under by the waves in the sea of this world.

Yes, because we are dealing with the world. The world that frequently surrounds us is the world Jesus referred to in his prayer for unity, the world in which we are, but to which we must not belong.

The foothold that enables us to continue our ascent towards the top of the mountain of perfection without falling, is the Word of Life.

This month, it says to us: "Let the man among you who has no sin be the first to cast a stone" (Jn. 8:7). Jesus said this to those who wanted to stone the adulteress. The central idea in Jesus' commands is always love. This is why he doesn't want us Christians to condemn anyone. In fact he says, "Do not judge," and proclaims, "Blessed are the merciful." Jesus wants mercy. Nevertheless, from what he says one could conclude that there *is* someone who could throw the first stone: whoever is without sin.

This is certainly no one of us; we are all sinners. But there is a person who is without sin. And we know who she is: the Mother of God. Could Mary, then, "throw a stone" at someone who erred? Did she ever do such a thing when she was on earth?

We know our Mother. We know what Scripture says about her, what Tradition has handed down to us about her, what the People of God have always thought about her: Mary loves everyone. She is merciful. She is the advocate of the most unfortunate. It is to her that countless Christians have turned, when they have had the impression that God's justice was upon them. Mary does not throw stones. Quite the contrary: no one except Jesus spreads love the way she does.

Why? Because she is a mother, and mothers only know how to love. It is typical of a mother to love her children as herself, because there's something of herself in them. I think that there's no better way for us to live this new Word of Life than to imitate Mary. We too can find something of ourselves in others. For we must see Jesus in ourselves and in every neighbor.

With each neighbor, at home, at work, or on the street; with the people we talk about; with those we speak to over the phone, or for whom we carry out our daily work — with every person we meet these next two weeks, we must think: "I must act *as if I were his or her mother*," and act accordingly. Mothers are always serving. Mothers always find excuses for their children. Mothers are always full of hope.

"As if I were his or her mother" — this is the thought which must be foremost in our minds these next two weeks. This must be our resolution, if we want to be sure not to throw stones: to be Mary's presence here on earth for everyone we meet.

Rocca di Papa, March 3, 1983

We are still living according to the Word: "Let the man among you who has no sin be the first to cast a stone" (Jn. 8:7). And to do this well, during these last few days we have looked to Mary, our Mother. She never judges, but always excuses her children, and keeps hoping till the very end. This Word of Life reveals the central message of the Gospel: God's love for humankind. God wants to save us, and for this reason he gave us his very own Son.

If this is how God loves people, then we must love in the same way. Besides everything else, this is how we live our vocation to the fullest, because love of neighbor is central to our spirituality. So, for the next two weeks, let's continue with this course of action; and we'll certainly take steps forward on the way towards sanctity. To encourage ourselves to practice this love which excuses everything, hopes in every circumstance, and believes all things, let's remember that one day it will have a decisive role to play in God's judgement of us.

Oftentimes, the thought of death is bitter to accept, because we are afraid of God's judgement. Not knowing what it will be like, we become frightened at the thought of our sins. If we believed Jesus' words, however, we would be able to influence the outcome of this judgement decisively, and we would have a pretty good idea of what to expect. Jesus says: "The measure with which you measure will be used to measure you" (Mt. 7:2), and "Blest are they who show mercy; mercy shall be theirs" (Mt. 5:7).

Our behavior toward our neighbor is *like a boomerang*, which, when thrown, comes back to us. Do we judge severely? A severe judgement will come back to us. Do we show mercy? Mercy will come back to us. When judging our neighbor, are we lenient, allowing him or her the benefit of the doubt? Then the same will happen to us. When dealing with our neighbor, do we try to find the good in the situation; make excuses; and certainly not set ouselves up as judges, even in the most obvious situations; but leave every verdict to God? If so, God will do the same for us.

During these next two weeks, let's deal this way with every neighbor we speak about, even those who pass beneath our gaze when we are reading the newspapers or looking at television — with ordinary people or with people in public life — with everyone. *The measure with which we measure will be used to measure us.*

Rocca di Papa, March 17, 1983

On Monday of Holy Week, our Holy Father, John Paul II, invited me to lunch. Eli[20] went with me. At the end of lunch, before saying goodbye, he gave us as a beautiful book about his fourteen trips, entitled, *Open the Doors wide to Christ*. What he said referring to this title showed the great trust he has in the Focolare. He said that the *focolarini* really put this exhortation of his into practice. We are certainly not worthy of such praise. However, we must act in a manner that will make us worthy of it.

"Open the doors wide to Christ." What does it mean? How can we do it?

I think that no one opens his or her heart wide to Christ, as well as those who open their hearts to the cross, to Jesus Crucified. It is our embracing the cross that allows us to experience the fullness of the life of the Risen Lord in us. This is a topic that we will analyze in depth another year, but that does not stop us from trying to understand it and live it right now.

The Risen Lord in our hearts! Certainly, whoever has the Risen Lord living in his or her heart, has opened that heart wide to the cross, to Jesus' cry of abandonment. One cannot speak of resurrection, in fact, unless there has been death.

During these next two weeks, we should discover where our cross awaits us in each present moment, open our heart wide, and embrace it. At times it might be an unexpected, personal suffering, or the suffering of someone near to us. Other times it might be one of the crosses related to our particular vocation: the barriers that arise because of differences in character; the disunity between Christians, or the feeling of distance that separates those of different faiths; the indifference of the individualistic and materialistic world that surrounds us. On other occasions, it might be the suffering involved in practicing virtues such as purity, patience, meekness, mercy, and so on. So let's open our hearts wide to all these crosses, and this will be the best way to open our hearts to Christ.

I was overjoyed a few days ago when I learned about the experience of a person who is on the Holy Journey with us. This person confided to me that two years ago — before these conference calls began — she had felt the desire to give Jesus the first place in her heart. At that time she felt that she had not done it yet. Now, after these years of striving towards sanctity, she feels that this aspiration is beginning to come true. She has noticed that in some moments of the day, Jesus is really the most important thing for her. And she attributes this to the fact that she has seriously tried to love Jesus Forsaken. Let's all try to do the same in these coming days: *Open our hearts wide to the cross, so as to open them wide to Christ.*

Rocca di Papa, April 7, 1983

START AGAIN FROM SCRATCH

Some time ago, Roger Schutz, the Prior of Taize, and I had a conversation in which he confided that meeting people from all over the world, especially young people, he had realized how much our world has been de–Christianized; to the point that he did not know anymore where to start to try to bring Jesus back to people.

To tell you the truth, this is often my own sad impression, too. Whereas thirty to forty years ago, our society (and here I am referring above all to Europe) was basically Christian, and therefore based on solid principles, today this is no longer the case. A secularized, materialistic mentality has crept in, and since the greater part of the human race thinks in a way that, for all practical purposes, is pagan, people believe that it is alright to act pagan. For example, we see the prevalence of divorce and abortion; of all sorts of premarital behavior, and people just living together without being married. All these things are considered normal ways of life, and therefore, people think that they are right.

People think: "Others don't do their work well; they take advantage of their neighbor; they rob from the government; so I can do it, too! Here you could list all the things that people's "old selves"[21] are doing that have made our world, an "old world." And it would be very interesting for us to list those subtle, little things that may have penetrated our behavior. For example, giving value to possessing things or to prestige; little things, such as attachments to countless material, or even spiritual things; the way we flee from sacrifice, from self-control, and so on.

The terrible thing is that this mentality has become so widespread and has penetrated so much, especially through the mass media, that we are immersed in it without even realizing it. And so we see the painful phenomenon of our young people sometimes candidly confessing that they do not know how to tell the difference between good and evil and don't know what sin is.

For some, as the Pope said recently, the word sin has become an empty expression. For others sin has been reduced to injustice. For others still, sin is an inevitable reality. Finally many interpret the moral law in an arbitrary way, even though they admit the existence of sin.

This is the situation, the grave situation in which we are living. How should we react? What should we do?

Faced with the anguished question of the Prior of Taize, I responded by saying that the only thing we can do is *start again from scratch*. And that's the way it is. We must begin as the first Christians began. They spread throughout the world in a short time, bringing the Gospel to many different peoples. They overcame the pagan world of their day, because two things were clear in their minds: that Christianity is, first of all, love—mutual love; and that they were *in* the world, but not *of* the world.

We too know that Jesus' message is love, and we really try to live it. Perhaps, however, we do not always have clear in our mind that although we are in the world, we cannot—must not—adopt its way of thinking. We are not of this world, not even of this twentieth-century world. We belong to a kingdom which is not of this world.

So let's continue to launch our revolution of love, and look at the world around us and everything that concerns it with a critical eye. The Word of Life this month, "Better for us to obey God than men" (Acts 5:29), can be a great help to us if we grasp its full meaning.

Yes, in the present moment, when the many pressures of the world would bend us to its way of thinking and acting, let's react forcefully. Let's allow our "new self," which appreciates the value of love, the other virtues, and the cross, to triumph in us. If in each of us, numerous as we are, our "new self" is victorious, then even a new world will not be unreachable. But we must have the zeal of the first Christians, and repeat everyday, every moment: "Better for us to obey God than men."

Rocca di Papa, April 21, 1983

Today, I'd like to encourage you once again to persevere in the Holy Journey. We must never stop, because as you know, "Whoever does not go forward, goes backwards." And since we frequently do stop, because we're sinners, we must develop the habit of saying to Jesus every time this happens: "Forgive me, I'm starting anew."

Starting anew to do what? Starting anew to live according to the Word of Life, because it is "a light for our path" and can enable us to bring our Journey to a happy conclusion and reach sanctity. Therefore, we must love God's word. It is enormously important for Christians.

During these last few days, I was quite struck by something Jesus says. After affirming that he has not come into the world to judge people but to save them, he says that there is something that will judge them on the last day: his word. When that terrible moment comes, will we find ourselves in conformity with his word; that is, will we be, as it were, his living words? If so, all will go well for us. But what if the opposite is true? Then his words will judge us.

Even if we do not take his words into consideration now, the moment will come when we will have to measure ourselves against them. So if love does not prompt us to live according to them, then at least fear should. Let us therefore love the Word, or at least have a holy fear of it. May's Word of Life encourages us to do this by telling us: "If anyone loves me, he will keep my word, and my Father will love him, and we shall come to him and make our home with him" (Jn. 14:23).

"If anyone loves me, he will keep my word." Jesus wants us to love his words. And if we do, he promises us something tremendous: the Trinity will come to dwell in us. So what "word" should we focus on during these next two weeks? Let's take one that sums up all the others.

Reading St. John of the Cross these past few months, I meditated on the description this unequalled mystic gives of all the steps in the soul's loving ascent to God, right up to the one called transforming union that concludes this journey towards sanctity. And I realized once again that *the secret of the saints*, the secret of their extraordinary experience, which was a true foretaste of heaven, was that they chose to embrace the cross. I believe that everything Jesus wants from us is concentrated in this choice. So, without reservations, let's renew our love for Jesus Forsaken, whom we encounter in the unexpected sufferings that come our way and in the struggle to conquer ourselves.

Rocca di Papa, May 3, 1983

BEARING FRUIT FOR THE
GLORY OF GOD

May continues to invite us to live Jesus' words, so that the Blessed Trinity may come to dwell in our souls. Therefore, I want to share something with you that came to mind recently while I was considering one of Jesus' teachings. I don't know if it happens to you, too, but every so often I feel a strong desire to have my life give glory to God, and wish I knew how to achieve this. Up to now, I have always found the answer in the writings of the saints, who assure us that whoever does God's will gives him glory and joy. Then, the other day, as I was following the readings of the Mass in my missal, I was deeply struck by a clarifying remark Jesus makes in St. John's Gospel: "My Father is glorified in this: that you bear much fruit and become my disciples" (Jn 15:8).

Reading this passage, I realized that through this conference call we have frequently encouraged one another to live its second part, which underscores the necessity of becoming Jesus' disciples. In fact, we often say that denying ourselves and carrying the cross are necessary conditions for following Christ. And we try to live accordingly. Up to now, however, we have not given the same emphasis to the first part of Jesus' statement, that is, the need to bear fruit; yet it is actually by living both parts that we give glory to the Father.

Today I would like to emphasize the necessity of bearing fruit. Here we immediately see the importance of a gift that all the Focolare members have—a typical way of bearing fruit, for which so many put forth their best efforts. This gift is the ability to share our "Ideal" with others by putting what we call "the technique of unity," into practice. One of the effects of this is the presence of Jesus in our midst, and he converts people's hearts, thus giving us the possibility of spiritually becoming mothers and fathers of souls.

Today, through the Gospel, Jesus confirms, that by doing this, we are really giving glory to the Father: "My father has been glorified in your bearing much fruit and becoming my disciples."

During the next two weeks we must commit ourselves to bear fruit, with the joy of knowing that by doing so we are giving glory to God. And we must take advantage of every chance we get, so that this fruit will be plentiful, as Jesus wants. This may involve renewing our love towards one or another of our neighbors, or getting in touch again with those we have lost contact with. Perhaps we will have to be more mindful of some of the persons in our cluster; or perfect "Operation One for One."[22] There will also be those who will feel the need to be more energetic in proclaiming the "Ideal" in new places.

Let's look into all the possibilities. Let's be generous with the time and energy we have, and let's be faithful. Every night, before we fall asleep, let's ask ourselves: "Did I bear fruit today? Much fruit?" If the answer is yes, then we can take comfort in it — we have given glory to God.

Rocca di Papa, May 19, 1983

BE PARTNERS AND BE SURE

If you drive along the roads of Switzerland these days, you will see big signs, very attractive ones. On them are two cars—one red, one blue— travelling along together. They smile and greet one another. The blue car signals with one hand for the red car to pass. The red car tips its hat in thanks. The motto on the sign says: "Be partners and be sure," which means that the surest way to have a safe trip is to help one another, to treat one another as partners, as friends.

I thought that this motto, if given a Christian meaning, could be true and helpful not only for journeys along the roads of this earth, but also for the Holy Journey that we have set out on. And for those who, like us, are called to follow the way of love, it is certainly the surest way, in fact, the obligatory way for us to reach our goal. All our obligations, are summed up in helping our neighbor. This is confirmed by the Word of Life for June, one of those sentences of Scripture centering on love, that touches a chord in us:"The whole of the Law is summarized in a single command: Love your neighbor as yourself" (Gal. 5:14 JB).

Thus, to strive towards sanctity means to focus all our attention, all our efforts, on loving our neighbor. For us, striving towards sanctity does not consist so much in trying to get rid of our defects one by one, but rather in loving, in thinking of others, completely forgetting ourselves. At the beginning of the Focolare, we used to say that there are two ways to have a clean room: you can either sweep the room you're in, or you can move into a clean room. We sensed that this second way was our way: to change rooms, that is, to no longer live turned in upon ourselves, but to be completely one with our neighbor, out of love.

But we know that whoever loves their neighbor, whoever lives for others, soon realizes that it is no longer they living, but Christ living in them. Jesus lives in their hearts. And who is Jesus? He is sanctity personified. We find sanctity in him, whose presence blossoms in us when we love. Sanctity comes as a consequence of loving, and we cannot attain it any other way. If we were to seek after sanctity for its own sake, we would never reach it.

Love then, and nothing else! Lose everything else, even the attachment to sanctity, so you can strive solely to love. Only in this way will we one day be able to give Mary the gift of our sanctity.

Let's start anew, as if today were the first day of our revolution of love, the first day of our Holy Journey. Let's love, without giving thought to anything else, because love sums everything. Let's live the next two weeks, trying to love every neighbor as ourselves; and to do this more successfully, let's live each individual situation fully.

Let's remember: *Be partners and be sure* — sure that what we are doing is the best thing we can do; sure that by acting this way, we are living according to our "Ideal"; sure of loving God, and of finding in our love for our neighbor, all the other virtues; sure that by doing this we can become saints. *Be partners and be sure!*

Rocca di Papa, June 2, 1983

All of us in the Focolare are still walking in the light of June's Word of Life: "The whole of the Law is summarized in a single command: Love your neighbor as yourself" (Gal. 5:14 JB).

During the last conference call, we were struck by this concise affirmation of Paul, and agreed that loving our neighbor sums up everything for us. Yes, everything. But why? Why is it, that when we love our neighbor, we feel completely fulfilled?

It's because, in loving our neighbor we find God; following the way that leads through our neighbor, we reach the Lord. And God is our Ideal. For forty years now, we have experienced that going to God through our neighbor is at times like going through a dark tunnel filled with pain, doubts, and anguish. It's rather like going through Purgatory, and then emerging to a clearer vision of Heaven, a deeper experience of the divine. Love for our neighbor leads inevitably to love for God.

This is what our "Ideal," the charism of the Focolare, has always pointed out to us. This is what the Church— whose decisions reflect God's will— confirmed, when, after studying at length the goals for which God had brought the Focolare into being, she declared that God is calling us to be "perfect in love."[23]

Therefore, we too are called to be perfect; and perfect means saints, but saints in loving. Some are called by God to become saints, to reach union with him, through prayer and contemplation; others through the practice of individual virtues; still others through preaching, and so on. These are all things which we must certainly not overlook. But our way, *the way* for us, continues to be love for our neighbor.

Yes, we must reach sanctity. We must make our lives a Holy Journey, but a Journey of love. Besides, the only way to work so "that all may be one," is to unleash a revolution of love! Isn't love the only thing capable of uniting people, of making them live as the Mystical Body? Without love, how could we have the Risen Lord among us? And without him, our spiritual and apostolic life would have no foundation. Certainly, we cannot think of the Focolare, without thinking of love, because our new life blossomed from our discovery of God as Love.

Our task, then, is to love. That is how we must seek our perfection. Moreover, we must always improve our love for each neighbor we encounter during the day: by taking particular care of the meal we have to prepare, or the lesson for the class we are going to teach, or the talk we have to write, or the affairs that we have to take care of, and so on. And if it seems to us that what we are doing is only to our own advantage — for example, going to school, in the case of the gens — let's keep in mind that we want to learn those subjects, or that art or profession, so we can be more useful in the future, to Jesus who is present in society.

We must do everything as well as possible, and should therefore listen carefully to the inner voice, whenever it offers us some suggestion or correction. Listen carefully, and do our best. When the saints reached the highest level of sanctity, which is called the transforming union, they had become completely one with Jesus, and thus possessed various gifts. One of these was the ability to perform perfect works.

From now on, let's make every effort to love as perfectly as possible, which means serving our neighbor perfectly. During these next two weeks, let's try to make our life a continuous act of *perfect service*.

Rocca di Papa, June 16, 1983

HEROIC LOVE, AND NOTHING LESS

When we last talked with one another, we decided to be more committed about loving our neighbor. And I've heard that the love this prompted many of you to have, is what made the recent Mariapolises, whose echoes have reached me from all over the world, so extraordinary. Today I'd like to speak to you again about love of neighbor.

What should our love be like, if it is to meet Jesus' expectations? We know: we must be ready to give our life for each and every neighbor. *Heroic love,* therefore, *nothing less!* This is love: "...as I have loved you." With this kind of love, we in the Focolare can become saints and make our lives a Holy Journey.

According to the spirituality of unity, if we love our neighbor like this, the whole of our spiritual life profits. And this is just what I've been discovering these past few days as I've tried to live this way. And I wanted to share this discovery with you.

You know that a spirituality is a way of living Christianity. It's a way of life, and life is made up of many things. In our spirituality, we usually speak about ten things in particular, which sum up all the rest. They are: God is Love, God's will, love of neighbor, mutual love, Jesus in our midst and unity, Jesus Forsaken, the Word of God, Mary, the Church, and the Holy Spirit.

These past few days, I've understood that by trying to have heroic love for my neighbor, I live all these other aspects of our spirituality a lot better. By loving my neighbor this way, I really have God, who is Love, for my Ideal, because I too am "love," in a small way. By loving my neighbor this way, I carry out God's will, which for me is summed up in love of neighbor. In fact, if I don't have love for my sisters and brothers at the basis of everything I do, anything I do will be worthless.

By loving this way, I do all my part to live in mutual love. Loving this way, I do everything I can to have Jesus in our midst, and to bring about unity. By loving my neighbor this way, I really love Jesus Forsaken, because I measure my love against his. If I love my neighbor like this, living according to the Word of Life will sooner or later become second nature, because each Word of Life helps me to love—*is* love—and reveals one of the many facets of love.

By loving this way, I really live like another Mary, because the way of love is her way: the *Via Mariae*[24] (Way of Mary), as we call it. And like Mary, not thinking of anything but love, I practice the virtues which loving implies: patience, mercy, obedience, poverty (because I am really giving), mortification (because I am thinking of others and not of myself), and so on. By loving this way, I live the Church and I live for the Church, because I contribute to unity, and unity "builds up" the Church; and through the Communion of Saints I help others to raise themselves spiritually. By loving this way, I give true honor to the Holy Spirit, because I obey him, by living the charism that he has given to me.

Let's love all our neighbors. Each encounter with our neighbor is a golden opportunity. Let's not neglect a single one of them in the course of our day. And let's love those whom we usually take into consideration because we have them right there beside us. Let's love those who perhaps escape our attention: those, for example, whom we speak about; whom we happen to remember; for whom we pray; about whom we hear something on the television or in the newspaper; those who write to us or to whom we write; all those for whom we do the work that we do every day.

Let's love the living, and those who are no longer on this earth. Let's love our neighbors individually and collectively; and, therefore, let's love and respect all peoples.

Let our love be heroic! Nothing less will do! We'll see the exceptional effects in our lives. We'll have light and happiness, and God's kingdom will be in us and among us, just as this month's Word of Life promises: "Do not live in fear, little flock. It has pleased your Father to give you the Kingdom" (Lk. 12:32).

Sierre, August 4, 1983

LOVE OF NEIGHBOR AND
THE TWELVE STARS

These last two weeks, I saw how intensely love of neighbor is being practiced throughout the Focolare, and the many effects it is having. In fact, reading the many telegrams which I received for my feastday,[25] I was overjoyed and consoled by the resolutions people had made, which revealed such supernatural enthusiasm and such burning love. It was a further confirmation that we are on the right track.

I have already told you how our whole spiritual life benefits from heroically putting love of neighbor into practice. Today, we will see that this is true, not only for people who live our spirituality, but also for those called to follow other spiritual ways. Love of neighbor leads them along the way of perfection, as well.

Remember the Twelve Stars of Perfection of St. John of the Cross? He says there are twelve stars that shine in the souls of those who have reached perfection and sanctity, having completed the Holy Journey, as we would say. These stars are: love of God, love of neighbor, chastity, poverty, obedience, private prayer, prayer in choir, humility, mortification, penance, silence, and peace. These past few days, I have noticed how loving our neighbor makes these twelve stars shine brighter in our souls. And to show you what I mean, let's review them quickly one by one.

Love of God. Does this love become more alive in our hearts when we love our neighbor? Certainly it does! It's like a plant: the deeper it sends its roots into the ground, the higher it grows towards the sun. The more we love our neighbor, the more God's love grows in us. That's the first star.

The second star is love of neighbor, which is exactly what we're doing.

The third star: chastity. The Focolare Rule states that the best safeguard of chastity is love of neighbor. And that's understandable: if you love, you think of others, and not of satisfying your own passions.

The fourth star: poverty. As we all know, we do not love poverty for poverty's sake. The characteristic of the Focolare members' poverty is that it is the result of sharing with our neighbor. We are poor in that we have only what is necessary because we give the rest to others, because in various ways, we share all that we possess with others.

The fifth star: obedience. Our first obedience is to God, to the charism the Holy Spirit has given us, which teaches us that our way to God is to love our neighbor. So by loving we are obedient.

The sixth star: private prayer. We know that our prayer life grows and deepens as our union with God grows. But this, in turn, increases, as we just said, when we love our neighbor. Thus, this star, too, shines brighter when we love.

The seventh star: prayer in choir. Love of neighbor stimulates us to pray together. When we truly love our neighbor as ourselves, and are one with him or her, don't we feel a desire — almost a need — to be united with him or her in prayer?

The eighth star: humility. True humility involves complete forgetfulness of self — annihilation of our ego — and this is accomplished perfectly when we love our neighbor, when we "live the other."

The ninth star: mortification. Loving our neighbor as Jesus wants, our self is not only mortified, but dead.

The tenth star: penance. The penance that God wants most from us, is the penance implicit in love of neighbor.

The eleventh star: silence. Loving our neighbor, we practice silence and avoid useless words. First of all, because to "make ourselves one," we have to silence everything in us. And this is the most sublime form of silence. Secondly, because, when we love, the Holy Spirit, the Source of love, is present in our hearts. The more we love, the stronger is his voice in us, which tells us, among other things, when we should speak and when we shouldn't.

The twelfth star: peace. Loving our neighbor, we acquire true peace, which is a fruit of the Holy Spirit, who is present wherever there is love.

So let's love. Let's keep loving all the time, so that in two weeks we may be able to see these twelve stars shining more brightly in us. If we love, it will happen. And we'll find that we've completed a good stretch of the Holy Journey. This is what I wish for you with all my heart.

Rocca di Papa, August 18, 1983

EVERY IDEA IS A RESPONSIBILITY

During these last conference calls, we have spoken about love for our neighbor. Today we want to turn from love, to the Author of love, to the one who puts this love in our hearts, the Holy Spirit.

Why? Because September's Word of Life tells us not to serve two masters, but one alone: God. God speaks to us in various ways. Among these are the inspirations of the Holy Spirit, who is God; just as the Father is God; just as the Word is God. This month, therefore, we must serve God by listening to the gentle voice of the Spirit, who speaks within us, and doing what he says.

I really wish that all of us members of the Focolare, might have a very special love for this God who is unknown to so many people. One of our distinguishing characteristics should be an ardent devotion to him; because, individually and collectively, we owe him a great debt.

For example, we often say how happy we are to have gotten to know our spirituality; that it has become the basis of our lives; that for ten or twenty or thirty years, we have been trying to live it. And we cannot deny, that during all this time, it has given not *a* reason, but *the* reason to our life, and to the lives of many, many others. It has filled us with light, it has allowed us to experience pure joy, it has put a smile on our face, and on the faces of many others, it has resolved our problems, it has brought us back to life, it has always given us hope, it has launched us on a unique, stupendous, divine adventure.

Now then, have we ever asked ourselves what we would be without this spirituality? Well let's ask, and we'll see how much more sadness, emptiness, boredom, and sense-lessness, and how much less fruitfulness there would be in our life. Now, who is it that has poured this new life into our hearts? Who keeps it alive? Who nourishes it, day by day, with new inspirations? The Holy Spirit, whom Jesus promised to his apostles as he was about to leave this earth.

He dwells in the hearts of Christians; and so he's here in my heart, in your hearts, in the hearts of our sisters and brothers. How ungrateful we are, if we don't love Him! It's extremely bad manners to always be receiving, and never give!

But at least we're still alive! We still have time to do something, so that when our Holy Journey ends, and we go to the next life and behold the Blessed Trinity, we won't have to be so embarrassed. September's Word of Life, as I said, gives us this opportunity.

The Holy Spirit dwells within us, and speaks to our hearts. So let's become attentive, determined pupils of this great Teacher. Let's listen carefully to his mysterious, gentle voice. Let's not overlook any idea that might be an inspiration from him.

At the beginning of the Focolare, we were greatly helped by putting into practice the motto, *"Every idea is a responsibility."* Let's remember that the ideas which come into the mind of a person who has decided to love, are frequently inspirations of the Holy Spirit. And why does he give them to us? For our own benefit, and so that, through us, the world might benefit; and so that we might continue our revolution of love.

Let's be on the alert, then! Let's take every idea—especially if we think it might be an inspiration—as a responsibility, to be carefully considered and put into practice. If we do this, we'll have found a very good way to love, honor, and thank the Holy Spirit, and to obey only one Master.

Rocca di Papa, September 1, 1983

HONOR THE HOLY SPIRIT

Last conference call, we spoke about the Holy Spirit. And I'd like to take up the same subject again today; so that by getting to know this "Unknown God" better, we may love, honor, and obey him.

The Holy Spirit can do incredible things! Just look at the Apostles! The Church had been founded by Jesus on the cross, yet they were dumbfounded, hesitant, scared, hiding behind locked doors. Then the Holy Spirit came down upon them, and they were filled with courage. They went out into the streets and squares, and spoke with such fire, that people thought they were drunk. Later, they bravely faced persecution and set out to bring the Good News to the whole world.

This is just one important example of what the Holy Spirit can do—not to mention all that he has done in the Church throughout her twenty centuries of life: miraculous outpourings of light, grace, transformation, and renewal. Think of the Councils, and of the various spiritual movements he raised up, always at just the right moment. Look at the Focolare. Isn't something of this sort also happening with us, because of the fact that the Holy Spirit has bestowed one of his charisms on us?

Before this happened to change our lives, weren't we just like all those people who don't see beyond their own neighborhood, whose thoughts and affections are limited almost exclusively to the small circle of their family; who are bent solely—as we were—on acquiring a profession, or on owning a car or a house; who try to brighten up their lives by going out to the movies or attending some sporting event on their days off?

Then the Holy Spirit intervened and gave us this wonderful new life. He helped us break out of our own self-centeredness, and start thinking about our neighbor. He gave us hope — and often proof — that, with his help, many of the problems that afflict the world could be resolved. He gave us the courage to speak in front of crowds, which we would never have imagined possible. He also gave us the strength to spiritually — and often literally — leave behind, not only our own neighborhood, but our own country and our own culture, to bring the fire of his love to the ends of the earth. He gave us the strength, day after day, to overcome difficulty and misfortune; and often with joyful hearts.

As a result, we have often experienced the Father's extraordinary providence; and we have seen the fruits of our labor: many people all over the world, united in one big family.

If, to a greater or lesser degree, things around us have changed for the better, this is the work of the Holy Spirit, who renews the face of the earth. Yes, for his task is to instill drive and motivation; to enable grace — the divine life Jesus has obtained for us — to operate in our lives; to give us strength and courage. Since we owe him so much, he should hold a much more prominent place in our spiritual lives.

Last time we focused on the fact that the Holy Spirit lives in our souls; that we are his temples; and that each of us must listen to his voice speaking within us. Today we want to focus on the fact that he is also present in the soul of every neighbor we meet, who is also a temple of the Holy Spirit, or destined to be one. If this is so, don't you think this is an added reason to love our neighbor even better? Just as we show the proper respect before a tabernacle where Jesus is present in the Eucharist; similarly, we must have proper respect for all our sisters and brothers, because they are tabernacles of the Holy Spirit.

Here, then, is a thought to illuminate our path in the days ahead: *Let's honor the Holy Spirit,* by loving, respecting, and serving every neighbor.

Rocca di Papa, September 15, 1983

THE POWER OF THE SPIRIT

I have received requests from all over, to say some more about the Holy Spirit, the God who, unfortunately, is often forgotten. And I am very happy to do this. After all, hasn't he always watched over us?

We already spoke about where we can find the Holy Spirit, to honor him, obey him, and show him our love. He is in our hearts, and so it is wise and helpful, if we want to have a successful Holy Journey, to always listen to his voice. He is present in each neighbor, as in a temple, and therefore we have been making every effort to love those around us twice as much.

But where else can we find him? It is good to know just where he is present, because we human beings are always rather materialistic, and so it is much easier for us to demonstrate our devotion to God when his great love allows us to see him and touch him — as in the Holy Eucharist, where Jesus is present under the appearances of bread and wine. We find it more difficult to express our devotion to him, when he remains what he truly is: pure Spirit, completely inaccessible to our senses — as in the case of the Holy Spirit.

In fact, the Holy Spirit is compared to the wind — at times forceful, at other times gentle. He is also represented by a dove, an animal we associate with lightness and gentleness, which flies about softly. It is said that the Holy Spirit blows wherever he pleases, and no one knows where he comes from, or where he is going.

But this gentle God, who is all love, acts powerfully. Just look at those individuals whom Jesus has decided should receive a special infusion of the Holy Spirit —

priests, for example: by the power of the Holy Spirit, they are able, with just a few words, to make God Himself present on the altar and to wipe away sins from people's hearts.

Look at the shepherds of the Church, the bishops: haven't we always found something in these chosen servants of the People of God, that we have never found in anyone else? Doesn't what they say touch our hearts? Doesn't it seem particularly enlightened? Even the statements of the best-prepared theologians are no comparison! Hearing their warm and comforting words, don't we feel enveloped by the Church's maternal love? And when they are present at our gatherings, aren't those moments the highpoints?

Since the Focolare began, haven't those of us who are Catholic recognized something unique and true in all that the different popes have said? Isn't that why their words are so precious to us?

Well, it is the Holy Spirit who does all this. He is the one who fulfills the words and promises of Jesus, filling the Church and its ministers with life, in every time and place.

We must be conscious of this special presence of the Holy Spirit in these people who are particularly called to bring Heaven to humanity, and humanity to Heaven. We must overcome the sometimes cold and icy atmosphere that secularism and materialism have spread everywhere; in which they are frequently banished from the mainstream of society, as if they were non-existent or unnecessary for the progress of modern life. We must always be ready, instead, to give them the place of honor that belongs to them, while avoiding outdated attitudes and modes of behavior.

The Word of Life this month says: "When you have done all you have been commanded to do, say, 'We are useless servants. We have done no more than our duty'" (Lk. 17:10). You have read in the commentary that, taken in context, these words express not so much the uselessness of what we do, but rather Jesus' concern that we be always mindful of the infinite distance there is between God and us, as between everything and nothing.

Well then, during the next two weeks, to be more aware of our nothingness and to honor the Holy Spirit, let's cultivate a special love for God's ministers; and try to remember the suggestions, admonishments, and directives they have given us, and put them into practice. Let's make a special effort to pray for them and to point out to others the good work they have done, defending them if they are criticized. This attitude, which Saint Francis of Assisi always had — even toward priests who had mistresses; to the point of kissing the ground where they had walked — will bring us many blessings, and the Holy Spirit will lavish new gifts upon us.

Rocca di Papa, October 6, 1983

"YOU ARE EVERYTHING, I AM NOTHING"

Today, let's again renew our resolve to strive for sanctity, which means to live our spirituality without hesitation, starting over again every time we fail.

As a light for our Journey, we have October's Word of Life: "When you have done all you have been commanded to do, say 'We are useless servants. We have done no more than our duty'" (Lk. 17:10).

As I mentioned last time, we can understand from the context, that with these words Jesus does not want to say that our actions are useless, but rather that we should always be mindful of the infinite distance that exists between God and us, as between everything and nothing. The saints, those great Christian men and women, were always aware of this; and the prayer to God that often welled up from their hearts was: "I am nothing and You are everything." The fruit of this was, that at a certain point in their lives, they found that their nothingness had been filled by the One who is Everything: God had entered their hearts with his fullness. Having made themselves nothing, they even participated in his glory. We should heed the example of these truly fulfilled Christians, and do as they did.

I remember that at the beginning of the Focolare, wanting to imitate the saints, we often used to go to Jesus in the tabernacle, and declare repeatedly that he was everything and we were nothing. We did this especially before speaking in public, so that it would not be ourselves giving the others empty human words, but God in us speaking to their hearts. And I can't forget how often he heard our prayer—so often, that I am sure this is one of the reasons why, from the very beginning, the Focolare has been continually spreading.

We must continue to have this attitude toward God, telling him at every opportunity that we are nothing and he is everything. But above all, we must show by our lives that we are convinced that, of ourselves, we are nothing.

Through the various spiritualities that have made the Church beautiful down through the centuries, the Holy Spirit has suggested many ways by which Christians can learn to "live" their nothingness. For some the way is to constantly strive to deny themselves and practice acts of mortification—sometimes great acts of mortification. Others strive to extinguish all their "appetites," desires, and so on, so as to experience the *"nada"* (nothing) St. John of the Cross speaks of.

As for ourselves, while we must be mindful of the need for self-denial, we must go about it in a particular way. We are to reach the experience of our own nothingness by focusing our attention on God and his will, and on our neighbor—making his or her worries, sufferings, problems, and joys, our own. In other words, by loving.

If we love in every present moment, then without realizing it, we are acknowledging our own nothingness. And, since we will be living our nothingness, our life will be affirming God's superiority; the fact that he is everything. Simultaneously, however, because we are nothing, as a result of loving in the present moment, God will immediately share himself with us; and so we will be nothing of ourselves and everything because of him.

So let's resolve for the next two weeks, to make God's will our will— his will insofar as we know it and have planned for it; and also his unforseen will, that is manifested to us day by day, hour by hour. If we live this way, it will no longer be just our prayers telling Him, *"You are everything, I am nothing,"* but our very lives will cry it out.

Rocca di Papa, October 20, 1983

The part of our spirituality which we want to emphasize this year focuses on Jesus Crucified and Forsaken, whom we regard as the key to the union of our souls with God. In fact, if we look at how we understood and lived our spirituality at the very beginning of the Focolare, we cannot help making an amazing discovery: We can experience the presence of the Risen Lord and the consequent outpouring of the gifts of his Spirit—life, light, peace, love, consolation, ardor, etc.—not only when there are two or more persons united in Jesus' name, but even when we are alone.

How? What's the price? Embracing Jesus Forsaken in each present moment.

This extraordinary experience prompted us to look deeper into the Scriptures and the Church's teachings. And they confirmed that it was true.

So we need to embrace Jesus Forsaken in each present moment. But where are we to find him? In the denial of self and the taking up of our cross, which the Christian life demands of us, if we want to follow Jesus.

Therefore, we need to say yes to Jesus Forsaken and quickly embrace every suffering that comes our way—in other words, our cross. But for love to triumph in our hearts, we also need to embrace the suffering that comes from our efforts to deny ourselves, and from the struggle against our selfishness and the so-called desires of the flesh (tendencies toward overeating, impurity, quarreling, jealousy, and so on).

Figures of the game

TIMED on our stop-watch the first half of the Dublin-Mayo match lasted 31 mins. 11 secs., but the second period was 36 secs. short, lasting 29 mins. 24 secs.

FIRST HALF.

3.33 —Throw-in.

3.38¼—Dublin point by K. Heffernan.

3.39½—Dublin point by N. Maher.

3.45¼—Dublin point by O. Freaney (free).

3.49 —Mayo point by J. Curran (free).

3.50½—Dublin point by O. Freaney (free).

3.56¼—Mayo goal by J. Curran.

3.57½—Dublin goal by O. Freaney.

4.00½—Mayo point by J. Curran (free).

4.4.11—Half-time.

   Score—Dublin 1-4, Mayo 1-2.

SECOND HALF.

4.16 —Throw-in.

4.18½—Dublin point by M. Whelan.

4.20 —Mayo point by J. Curran (free).

4.24¾—Mayo point by J. Curran (free).

4.27½—Dublin point by O. Freaney (free).

4.34¼—Dublin point by O. Freaney.

4.36 —Dublin point by K. Heffernan.

4.38 —Mayo point by J. Curran.

4.42 —Mayo point by J. Curran (free).

4.44 —Mayo point by J. Curran (free).

4.45.24—Final whistle.

   Result—Dublin 1-8, Mayo 1-7.

DUBLIN

	Goals	Points	Wides	"50s"	Frees
First Half	1	4	4	1	9
Second Half	0	4	1	0	6
Total	1	8	5	1	15

MAYO

	Goals	Points	Wides	"50s"	Frees
First Half	1	~	3	0	18
Second Half	0	5	6	1	13
Total	1	7	9	1	31

Ireland from the ends of the earth—our own exiles in particular—and they were anxious to see places associated with Irish history.

They owed it to these people to have that place in a condition which they could all be proud.

One of the lessons of the fate of Clonmacnois was that force achieved nothing—that the spirit would always triumph.

Turf saved parish

Fr. O'Donohoe, who presided, said experience had shown that it was impossible to administer Clonmacnoise without Government intervention.

The parish of Clonmacnoise had, he said, suffered severely from emigration, but the coming of Bord na Mona had saved it from extinction.

"We should thank those men of vision who, twenty years ago, concentrated their attention on the bogs and marshes of the country which are now becoming the centres of life and industry with work provided in plenty and new houses beside it," he added.

Among the guests were: Mr. T. F. O'Higgins, Minister for Health; Mr. M. Donnellan, Parliamentary Secretary to the Minister for Finance; Mr. O. Flanagan, Parliamentary Secretary to the Minister for Agriculture; Rev. P. Barden, C.C., Clonfanbough; Rev. Fr. Aloysius, O.F.M., Athlone.

Plastics entering men's fashions

Plastics are giving a helping hand to men's fashions no Latest development is a pla

ALLY
PID
EF

DITY
RTBURN

If, in the present moment, these efforts are loved out of love for Jesus Crucified; and if, immediately afterwards, we do what God wants from us in that moment, we can experience the fullness of the life of the Risen Lord, even when we are alone.

Then his light comes into our hearts. His peace fills us. His love is enkindled in us, and with it, consolation, serenity, a taste of Heaven. In other words, everything changes. The soul is clothed anew, just as November's Word of Life, taken from St. Paul, says: "Put on the Lord Jesus Christ and make no provision for the desires of the flesh" (Rom. 13:14). That's what we want to do for the next two weeks: love Jesus Forsaken always, immediately, and joyfully; not only in our daily sufferings, but also in the effort involved in overcoming ourselves.

When Igino Giordani wrote the following poem, shortly after he had embraced our spirituality, that's precisely what he meant:

"I have set about dying
and what happens no longer interests me.
I have begun to find my joy
in Jesus' desolate heart."

He was speaking of dying to self, so as to rejoice with Jesus; of dying with the forsaken Jesus, so as to live with the risen Jesus.

So let's remember these words: *"I have set about dying."* And let's welcome the death of our own self—ten times, a hundred times a day, so as to give those we meet the joy of encountering the Risen Lord.

Rocca di Papa, November 3, 1983

The annual meeting of the European *focolarini*, at which some *focolarine* were also present, took place at the Mariapolis Center, from December 7th, the vigil of the Immaculate Conception, to December 10th, the feast of Our Lady of Loretto. The meeting was characterized by the joy which comes from Jesus and which is a gift of the Holy Spirit. This joy, impossible to contain, burst forth from the 700 hearts of those present. The meeting concluded with something special: we made a pact, promising that every morning, united in spirit, we would turn our hearts to Jesus Forsaken and offer him, as with one voice, a very special prayer. Today, as I was thinking that I would be speaking to all of you — *focolarini*, priests, volunteers, religious, gens, families, people committed in the Parish Movement, and so on — out there on the front lines, in this divine adventure of making Love more fully known in this world, I felt in my heart a desire to share with you this small but very important step we had taken.

As you know, we are now celebrating the 40th Anniversary of the beginning of the Focolare. And our thoughts cannot help but go back to the first days of this new life of ours. This year, moreover — in which the whole Focolare is going deeper into the reality of Jesus Forsaken as the key to the union of our souls with God — we cannot help recalling once again, that well-known episode at the beginning, when those of us in the first Focolare household gave everything we possessed, keeping only the mattresses on which to sleep on. We left but a single object hanging on the wall: a picture of Jesus Forsaken. We did this to show him our preferential love — or better, our exclusive love.

Before him each morning we would pray with these words: "Because you are forsaken...."

But what did those four words mean? Was it simply: *"Because you were forsaken, I now have life; and therefore I want to have you as the only reason for my life. And since I have made this choice, I want to love you in suffering; and in my neighbors, whose sufferings remind me of you, and in those persons and situations that we sense have something to do with the goals of this new Movement?"*

No. This was not the first meaning of that prayer. With those words we wanted to tell Jesus, *"Because you were forsaken, and by this saved us; because I, too, have died and risen with you — here I am, completely renewed, just as you want me to be, ready for this day! In every moment of this day, I will be the answer to your 'Why?' I will be a fruit of your abandonment. And not just any sort of fruit, but a worthy fruit: beautiful, full, tasty, at its peak. And, therefore, it is not enough for me to have received through baptism the faith and life which you merited for me by your cross and abandonment. I want to correspond fully to these gifts. So here I am, Jesus!"* In other words, we wanted to declare: *"Because you were forsaken, here I am!"*

This very month, the Word of Life says to us: "If you are repentant, produce the appropriate fruit" (Mt 3:8 JB). Certainly, all acts of love are "appropriate fruits." But, I'd like to invite all of you to join me in this prayer to Jesus Forsaken, and, if possible, to do something more for him: to be worthy fruits yourselves; and to say to him every morning, repeating it throughout the day with your lives, "Because you were forsaken, *here I am!*"

On the back of that picture of Jesus Forsaken, as many of you know, was written: "My vineyard is always before me" — as if these words had been said by Jesus. During these next two weeks, we must become the incarnation of these words. You, I, the 700 *focolarini*, the 50,000 or more all over the world who are linked up to this conference call — all of us must present ourselves before Jesus as worthy fruits. And I'm sure that none of you will miss this opportunity. He has loved us. We must love him back!

Rocca di Papa, December 15, 1983

1984

SETTING THE COMPASS

The Christmas meeting for the more-than-eight-hundred European *focolarine* also concluded with a little pact, which I want to tell all of about today. But first I want to share with you something I shared with them.

In the past I've pointed out that the call to follow Jesus Forsaken exclusively, did not simply take place once and for all at the beginning of the Focolare. From time to time, down through the years, the Lord has reinforced that call through particular episodes or intuitions. What follows happened to me in 1954. It's well-known, but useful to remember.

1954 was an important year for us: for the first time a *focolarino* was going to become a priest. I had to go from Rome to Trent for the ordination of Father Foresi by the Archbishop of Trent. Not being well, it seemed wise to travel most of the way by plane. As soon as I stepped aboard, a very kind stewardess — wishing to make the trip easier for me — invited me into the cockpit. There I was immediately struck by the magnificent view, wide and unobstructed, offered by the large cockpit windows. It was not the panorama, however, which struck me the most, but rather the brief explanation that the pilot gave me as to what is important in flying an airplane. He told me that if you want to have a straight, sure flight, first of all you must set the needle of your compass in the direction of your destination. Then, all along the way, you must keep an eye on it to make sure that the plane does not go off course.

As I was listening to this explanation, I immediately began to make a mental comparison between an airplane trip and the journey of life, which today I would refer to as the Holy Journey. It seemed to me that in life, too, we had to set our "compass," at the outset, in the direction our soul was to follow—which is Jesus Forsaken. Then, all along the journey, we had to do only one thing: remain faithful to Him.

Yes. The way which God calls us to follow is this, and this alone: to love Jesus Forsaken in every moment. This means embracing all the sufferings in our own life. It means putting love into practice, by always adhering to his will; doing away with our will, so as to let his will prevail. To love Jesus Forsaken means to discover what true love is, to learn what it means to love our neighbors—that is, to love them to the point of being forsaken, as he did. To love Jesus Forsaken in every moment, means to practice all the virtues, which he did heroically in that moment, for all to see.

December 31, 1983 marked the third anniversary of our Holy Journey, and we asked ourselves, "How far have we gotten?" We felt a very strong desire not to waste any more time. Well, I think I can say, that setting the needle of our spiritual compass in the direction of Jesus Forsaken is the best possible step we could take to assure the continuation and completion of our Holy Journey; and it will make our Journey easier, as well.

On that plane, I had noticed that the pilot was very free in his movements, because he used no reins, as you would need with a horse; nor steering wheel, as you would need in a car. Similarly, if we set the needle of our spiritual compass in the direction of Jesus Forsaken, we too will not need anything else to reach the goal safely. Just as in a plane there are no curves to take you by surprise, because you fly in a straight line; and you don't have the problem of mountains, because you quickly reach a good altitude;

so too, in our Holy Journey, our love for Jesus Forsaken immediately places us at a good altitude. Thus we are not frightened by unforeseen circumstances, nor tired out by climbing; because in Jesus Forsaken, whatever is unforeseen, difficult, or painful has already been foreseen, and has become what we are waiting for.

So let's set our compass on Jesus Forsaken; and then let's remain faithful to him. How? In the morning, as soon as we wake up, let's point the needle of our compass toward Jesus Forsaken, with our *"Here I am!"* that I spoke to you about last time. Then, during the day, from time to time, let's check our compass and see if we're still on course with Jesus Forsaken. If we find we're not, then, with another *"Here I am!"* let's get back on the right course, and we will be able to continue our Journey. This is the pact I made with the *focolarine*; this is the invitation I offer all of you today.

If we travel life's journey in the company of Jesus Forsaken, we too will be able to repeat with Pina[26], the famous words of St. Clare: "Go confidently, my soul, because you have a good companion for your journey. Go, because the One who has created you, has always watched over you, and has sanctified you."

This way, we will also live to perfection January's Word of Life, which says: "And I—once I am lifted up from earth—will draw all men to myself" (Jn. 12:32). And we will reap fruits, fruits, and more fruits for the cause: "That all may be one."

Rocca di Papa, January 5, 1984

Two conference calls ago, we agreed that we would start our day by saying to Jesus Forsaken, as our first prayer each morning: "Here I am!" meaning that we had decided, that from the first moment of each day, we would be a worthy, beautiful, ripe fruit of his abandonment, of his redemption.

At the time of our last phone call, we decided to set the needle of our spiritual compass on Jesus Forsaken, so that during the course of the day we would not deviate from our firm resolution to love him.

What's the next step we should take in our Holy Journey?

You know that the Lord has given us an extraordinary charism, which truly focuses on the essence of Christianity. Because of this gift, we understood from the very beginning, that we were called to love — to live according to Jesus' New Commandment, to share in the Love (*Agape*) which is God himself: "God is love" (1 Jn. 4:8). And this must continue to be the focus of our life, our constant point of reference. This is the great revolutionary reality we are called to offer to today's tension-filled world, as well as to the Christian world still traumatized by division; just as the early Christians offered it to the world of their time.

The New Commandment is our vocation: Jesus himself referred to it as "his" and called it "new" to emphasize its importance (even though his other commands were also his and also new). And the early Christians, as we see in St. John, considered it the good news par excellence.

The New Commandment—this is our calling: a vocation to love, to love in every moment; to enkindle a blaze of love in the world; to be constantly ready each day to pay our "debt,"—as St. Paul puts it—our debt of love (cf.Rom. 13:8). The Spirit, who is present in each one of us and has made us free, pours love into our hearts and leads us to love others—to put ourselves at their service, to consider every person we meet our master.

But who can teach us this way of loving, which involves such complete self-denial? Who can teach us this kind of love, which leads us, in each present moment, to fulfill our obligation as Christians, and at the same time leads us toward perfection—toward sanctity—more effectively than anything else; more than penance, even more than vows?

We know the answer: Jesus Forsaken on the cross. He is our "style" of loving. This is how he loved humanity; this is how we should love our fellow human beings.

So here's a good suggestion for the next two weeks: Whenever we encounter another person—at work, at school, at home, while shopping, or anywhere else; whenever we speak with someone on the phone, or whenever we mention someone in conversation, let's be especially ready to say "Here I am!" to Jesus Forsaken, ready to give up everything, to "make ourselves one" with that person.

"Here I am, Jesus Forsaken, ready to love you in every encounter with another person." This is our commitment; this is the straightest way to the goal. This is the thrust we have to maintain all day long, if we want to put this month's Word of Life into practice: "And I—once I am lifted up from earth—will draw all men to myself" (Jn. 12:32). If we do this, the next two weeks will be a time of unimagined spiritual progress and unexpected conversions to Christ.

Rocca di Papa, January 19, 1984

If there's a problem today that everyone's concerned about, it's the problem of peace. It's so important that no one can choose to ignore it. Heads of government, as well as the Holy See, are working to establish relationships to help maintain peace, wherever it still exists. Both religious and secular movements are doing all they can through meetings, marches, publications, and so on, to keep the issue alive in people's minds. But each individual Christian should also be aware that he or she is in a unique position to contribute to the cause of peace.

What the Pope said in his Peace Message is quite true: "We need to undergo a change of heart, to have a new heart." This is something we Christians have a special grace to do. And it is a particularly serious obligation for us members of the Focolare, since we focus so much on the words of the Gospel.

The Word of Life for February tells us: "If you bring your gift to the altar and there recall that your brother has anything against you, leave your gift at the altar, go first to be reconciled with your brother, and then come and offer your gift" (Mt. 5:23).

This command constituted one of the fundamental causes of the real "revolution" which took place in the city of Trent at the beginning of the Focolare, surprising and converting many people. One reason was that these words made clear that God preferred love of neighbor over offerings to him, and that he was not pleased with the gifts of people who oppress the poor. But this was not the only reason.

These words had such surprising effects, because in trying to live them to the letter, taking them at face value, we understood what was so new about them. After all, the Old Testament had already affirmed that God rejects as hateful, the sacrifices of those who oppress their neighbors. But the reason this Word of Life had such powerful effects and changed so many situations, was that it made us realize that wherever there is tension, disharmony, or disunity, Jesus demands that not only the guilty party try to remedy the wrong done, but that even the one who has been wronged should do the same. In fact, he says: "If your brother has something against you," not, "If you have something against your brother." Thus, we understood, that as soon as any one of us noticed that the unity and harmony among us had diminished and was no longer having its extraordinary effects, we ourselves had to do something about it. Throughout the forty years since then, our efforts to live this way are what has maintained such a strong unity within the Focolare.

So this Word of Life is extremely helpful for living in unity, which, in turn, is a guarantee of peace — true peace in people's hearts. To put it into practice, we really need to have a new heart — not looking at who is right or who is wrong, but, because we are Christians, always seeing to it that perfect unity is maintained among us.

What should we do, then, during these next two weeks to put this Word of Life into practice to the fullest? Let's each look first of all at our own personal situation. All of us have relatives with whom we are in close contact, friends at school, or at work, people to whom we report, people entrusted to us in our clusters, neighbors we meet day after day. Does some relative have something against us for one reason or another? Have some friends criticized us for being Christian, or members of the Focolare? Is there someone who has asked us to do something for them, and is now beginning to get upset with us because we still haven't done it? Could it be that even in our own gen unit, volunteer nucleus or even Focolare household, something has happened to disrupt the harmony among us? Or is this unity and harmony growing weaker because one of us is contributing very little to it? Whether all this is our fault, or somebody else's fault, let's not rest till we have remedied the situation.

This is a must! It's obligatory! We are Christians; we are members of a movement whose full name is: the Focolare of Unity. *Unity must come before everything else.* The "gifts" to God—prayers, works of charity, and so on—come afterwards, after we have reestablished unity. If it is really not possible to reestablish unity first, we can still pray or go to Mass; but we must promise Jesus that we will fulfill this obligation as soon as possible.

Imagine if everyone lived like this—and not just single individuals, but countries, too! Imagine if even just the Christians of the world—all one billion of them—lived like this! Peace would certainly not be a problem anymore.

So let's live like this for the next two weeks. Let's say, "Here I am!" before every situation which is crying out for a solution. "Here I am!"—for love of Jesus Forsaken, who clothed himself with disunity to reunite everyone.

Rocca di Papa, February 2, 1984

IT IS ALSO LOVE TO ASK

We are still being inspired by the Word of Life: "If you bring your gift to the altar and there recall that your brother has anything against you, leave your gift at the altar, go first to be reconciled with your brother, and then come and offer your gift" (Mt. 5:23).

These words have made clear to us once again, the place and importance that Jesus gives to mutual love. I was happy to hear that in some places all the Focolare members immediately began to work at clearing up unresolved situations, small disunities, and longstanding grudges. We can really thank God! Let's continue! With this Word of Life, Jesus has told us clearly that there can be no union with God, real worship, or authentic prayer, unless we are reconciled with our brothers and sisters. So let's hope that his message has entered deeply into our hearts. It is with this hope, that I would like to speak to you about prayer, which, if we live this way, is certainly acceptable to God. I would like to speak, in particular, about the prayer of petition: that is, our asking for help and for favors. I have the impression that some of us may not stress it enough, even if for very noble reasons. Now that we have become more deeply involved in our Faith and begun to practice our religion much more, we have understood that religion is not simply a matter of going to church and repeatedly asking for things; but of loving God, and therefore, of giving. And to do our part, as we say, we have committed ourselves to living out all those principles of the Gospel that our spirituality emphasizes. Certainly this is all well and good. Nonetheless, we must realize that loving God means many things. It implies keeping *all* his commands. And one command that Jesus repeats insistently, is to ask: "Ask and you will receive. Seek and you will find. Knock and it will be opened to you" (Mt. 7:7). So, what should we do, then? We should ask more, and ask in a better way, because this is what Jesus wants. It's another way to show him our love.

Look, we've been traveling on our Holy Journey for more than three years now, and it would be wise to pause every so often and reflect on how things are going: to see if we have made progress, or whether we feel that we haven't gotten anywhere, or if we've lost our initial thrust. We might ask ourselves, "Why is it that in spite of all the supernatural light I have received compared to so many other people; in spite of so much encouragement from by brothers and sisters; in spite of all the promises and resolutions I have made; I am still so slow and so lacking in generosity when it comes to loving and practicing virtue — even when it comes to fighting temptations? Isn't what I have been able to do, completely out of proportion to all that I have received; and even to what I myself have resolved to do?" The best answer to these questions is given to us by Jesus: "Apart from me you can do nothing" (Jn. 15:5), which means: "In spite of all your efforts, your beautiful meditations, the encouragements, and good resolutions, you don't make much progress because you don't pray enough, because you don't ask for the help you need."

Saints have said that those who pray will be saved, and those who don't will be damned. Therefore, it is clear that those who pray, go forward spiritually; and those who don't pray at best remain at a standstill, but usually go backward. I know that all of you pray. The *focolarini* pray more than two hours a day. The others dedicate various amounts of time according to their vocation. I know, that from the youngest on up, you pray *"consenserint's"*[27] — as we say — on every important occasion: when someone is born or dies, when someone marries or consecrates their lives to God, when there are extraordinary situations to face. Certainly we pray and that means we don't rely only on our strength. Still, we can improve in two directions: first of all, not by multiplying the number of our prayers, but by becoming more fully aware of what we are already asking for. Reflect for a moment, and you will see how many graces we ask for in our morning and evening prayers, during Mass, in our thanksgiving after Mass, when we pray the rosary, and when we meditate.

Secondly, we can improve — as the saints point out — by praying in such a way that we receive what we ask for. Our prayers are heard if we ask with humility, aware that we can do nothing on our own; with trust, confident that with God we can do anything; and with perseverance, lovingly insistent, as Jesus wants us to be. In short, we must focus on the requests that we already make, give them greater attention, and express them better each time, praying with the same effort that we put into living the rest of our spirituality. In this way, everything we do will be more fruitful. And let's pray while we still have time! I always remember the advice given us by the mother of one of the first *focolarine* just before she died: "Pray during your life, because at the end, you won't have time."

So then, for the next two weeks let's focus on prayer, let's become aware of all that we ask for, and ask it with all our hearts, out of love for God.

Rocca di Papa, February 16, 1984

NOTES

1. Speaking to 1000 gens on New Year's Eve, 1980, the author referred to Sister Maria Gabriella, an Italian Trappistine nun who had offered her life to God for Christian unity. During the last three years of her life, she had managed to master her own difficult character and to reach Christian perfection. (She was beatified by John Paul II on January 25, 1983.) The author pointed to her as an example, and urged the gens to set out on the Holy Journey and to reach sanctity as quickly as possible.
2. See Introduction.
3. The practice of "making ourselves one," as St. Paul did, is a key point of Focolare spirituality. For a full explanation see *May They All be One* (New York: New City Press, 1984).
4. Another key point of Focolare spirituality is mutual love—the living out of Jesus' "New Commandment" (Jn. 13:34; 15:12) so as to merit Jesus' presence as he promised: "Where two or three are gathered in my name, there am I in their midst" (Mt. 18:20).
5. See Introduction.
6. The number of people in the Focolare who, at that time, were receiving the message of the conference calls.
7. The author is referring to an image that, on another occasion, she explained as follows: "We in the Focolare should be grouped in clusters: each one of us who lives our Gospel spirituality, with a group of others who are doing the same—so that we will all have greater strength, determination, and zeal to carry on the Holy Journey and reach sanctity. And each of us

should feel responsible for a cluster of our brothers and sisters whom God has entrusted to us; and we should love them, serve them, and help them." This image is also one used by the early Christians (Cf. Papia, *The Life of St. Ireneus*).

8. Heavenly Mariapolis: This expression is sometimes used in the Focolare to mean the next life. It derives from "Mariapolis" (City of Mary), name of the Focolare summer gatherings. (See list of Focolare terms on page 9.)

9. A gathering of 7000 priests and religious men belonging to, or associated with the Focolare, which was held in Paul VI Hall, Vatican City, on April 30, 1982.

10. The image of the vineyard is taken from Scripture (cf. Ps. 80:9-17; Is. 27:2-3). Here the author uses it to refer to the Work of Mary, considered as a fruit of Jesus' abandonment on the cross.

11. Radi Follador, Italian *focolarina* who died on April 19, 1982.

12. *Novissima Verba*: The Last Conversations and Confidences of St. Thérèse of the Child Jesus. New York: P.J. Kennedy & Sons, 1952.

13. The image of the kangaroo, which the author first used when speaking to younger members of the Focolare in Australia, brings out the determination, willpower, and quick spiritual reflexes needed in overcoming obstacles in the spiritual life, so as to go forward spiritually with a minimal expenditure of energy, like a kangaroo does, physically. This lesson, in addition to being good psychology, reflects sound principles of moral and spiritual theology.

14. Loppiano: The first permanent Mariapolis (see Some Focolare Terms on page 9), located south of Florence, Italy.

15. cf. *Spunti di amore*, 77, in *Opere* (Roma, 1979), p. 1101.

16. "Let me hear what God the Lord will speak,
    for he will speak peace to his people,
    to his saints, to those who turn to him in their hearts."
    (Ps. 85:8 RSV)

17. A visual aid previously used by the author to help the younger members of the Focolare to understand our ascent to sanctity together. (See message of January 7, 1982.

18. The author has often spoken of her desire to offer Mary all the effort involved in striving toward Christian perfection by practicing the spirituality of the Focolare.

19. John XXIII, *Journal of a Soul*, trans. Dorothy White (New York: McGraw-Hill, 1965), p. 98.

20. Eli Folonari is one of the author's early companions in the Focolare.

21. "You must lay aside your former way of life and old self..." (Eph. 4:22); "What you have done is put aside your old self with its past deeds and put on a new man, one who grows in knowledge as he is formed anew in the image of his Creator" (Col. 3:9-10).

22. This expression was coined by the author to stimulate the Focolare members to involve at least one other person in living the Gospel more fully.

23. The general aim of the Focolare is that its members become "perfect in love." The reference here is to the Rule of the Focolare, approved by the Catholic Church in 1962.

24. The spiritual way followed by Focolare members and inspired by the Gospel events in the life of Mary.

25. In Italy, people celebrate the feast of their patron saint as we celebrate birthdays in the United States.

26. Pina de Vettori. One of the early *focolarine*, who died on January 5, 1984.

27. *consenserint*: This Latin word is used in the Focolare to indicate a form of prayer recommended by Jesus, and widely used by the Focolare members: "Again I tell you, if two of you *join your voices (consenserint)* on earth to pray for anything whatever, it shall be granted you by my Father in heaven" (Mt. 18:19).

HIGHLIGHTS IN THE HISTORY
OF THE FOCOLARE

1943 - Chiara Lubich consecrates her life to God
1944 - First women's Focolare household: Trent, Italy
1948 - First men's Focolare household: Trent, Italy
- Igino Giordani becomes first married *Focolarino*
1949 - First Mariapolis (Focolare summer gathering): Italy
1956 - The branch of the "Volunteers for God" begins — First
Focolare household outside Italy: Brussels, Belgium
1958 - First Focolare households outside Europe:
Brazil and Argentina
1959 - Last single Mariapolis in Italy: 12,000 participants
1960 - Centro Uno Ecumenical Center opens in Rome
1961 - Inauguration of International School of Formation
for *focolarini*: Rome
- First Focolare households in North America:
New York
1962 - Pope John XXIII officially approves the Focolare,
under the name "Work of Mary"
1963 - First Mariapolis in North America: New Jersey
1964 - Inauguration of the International School of
Focolare Spirituality for Diocesan Priests: Rome
- Chiara Lubich visits Focolare households
in North America
- First permanent Mariapolis founded: Loppiano,
Italy
1966 - Permanent Mariapolis begins in Fontem,
Cameroon
- The Archbishop of Canterbury, Michael Ramsey,
receives Chiara Lubich in audience, and encourages
the spreading of the Focolare in the
Anglican Church

- First Focolare households in Asia: Manila, Philippines
- First Focolare household in Australia

1967 - First of many audiences of Chiara Lubich with Patriarch Athenagoras I in Istanbul
- The Gen Movement (youth section of the Focolare) begins

1968 - Chiara Lubich visits the Focolare households in New York and Chicago. She founds the school of formation for American *focolarini*
- Mariapolis Center (for the Focolare meetings and retreats) is inaugurated in Chicago
- Permanent Mariapolis begins in O'Higgins, Argentina

1969 - Inauguration of the Center for Ecumenical Life at Ottmaring, Germany
- Permanent Mariapolis begins near Sao Paolo, Brazil

1970 - Inauguration of the International School of Focolare Spirituality for Women Religious: Rome

1973 - First Gen Fest: Loppiano, Italy. 3,000 participants

1974 - Permanent Mariapolis begins in Tagaytay, Philippines

1977 - Chiara Lubich is awarded the Templeton Prize for Progress in Religion
- Inauguration of the International School of Focolare Spirituality for Men Religious: Rome
- Two Mariapolises take place in North America: Oregon and New York

1978 - Three Mariapolises take place in North America: Washington State, New Mexico, and New York

1980 - Fourth Gen Fest: Rome. 50,000 participants

1981 - Family Fest: Rome. 25,000 participants
- Chiara Lubich is honored with the Order of Saint Augustine of Canterbury by the Archbishop of Canterbury, Robert Runcie, for her work "within and for the Anglican communion"

- Inauguration of Ecumenical Schools for the members of the Focolare in Great Britain, Germany, and the United States
- Permanent Mariapolis begins in Montet, Switzerland
- Chiara Lubich speaks about her Christian experience before 10,000 Buddhists in Tokyo, Japan
- Four Mariapolises take place in North America: Washington State, New Mexico, Wisconsin, and New York
- The Focolare in North America celebrates its twentieth anniversary at a commemorative Mass in St. Patrick's Cathedral, New York, with 2,000 attending. Cardinal Cooke is main celebrant

1982 - World congress of 7,000 priests and men religious associated with the Focolare takes place in Paul VI Hall, Rome. Participants from sixty countries. Pope John Paul II addresses them and is main celebrant at Mass described as largest concelebration in history

1983 - Inauguration of the Asian branch of the School of Focolare Spirituality for Diocesan Priests: Tagaytay, Philippines
- International conference of the New Humanity Movement of the Focolare: Rome.
Pope John Paul II addresses 20,000 participants

1984 - Chiara Lubich is honored with the Byzantine Cross by the Ecumenical Patriarch of the Orthodox Church, Demetrius I
- Pope John Paul II visits the international headquarters of the Focolare in Rocca di Papa, Rome